WILD ABOUT
PLANET EARTH

WILD ABOUT
PLANET
EARTH

WRITTEN BY
ANNA CLAYBOURNE, CLARE OLIVER, PETER RILEY

Little Hippo
Books

First published in 2019 by Miles Kelly Publishing Ltd
Harding's Barn, Bardfield End Green, Thaxted, Essex, CM6 3PX, UK

Copyright © Miles Kelly Publishing Ltd 2019

2 4 6 8 10 9 7 5 3 1

Publishing Director Belinda Gallagher
Creative Director Jo Cowan
Editorial Director Rosie Neave
Cover Designer Simon Lee
Designers John Christopher (White Design), Venita Kidwai, Elaine Wilkinson
Image Manager Liberty Newton
Indexer Michelle Baker
Production Controller Elizabeth Collins
Reprographics Stephan Davis
Assets Venita Kidwai

Consultants Clive Carpenter, Steve Parker, Clint Twist

ISBN 978-1-960009-31-9

Printed in China

Made with paper from a sustainable forest

littlehippobooks.com

Contents

PLANET EARTH

1 The Earth is a huge ball of rock moving through space at nearly 2,000 feet per second. It weighs 6,000 million, million, million tons. Up to two thirds of the Earth's rocky surface is covered by water—this makes up the seas and oceans. Rock that is not covered by water makes up the land. Surrounding the Earth is a layer of gases called the atmosphere (air). This reaches to about 620 miles above the Earth's surface— then space begins.

▶ Earth and the planets nearest to it in the Solar System. Mercury is the smallest planet. Venus is a similar size to Earth, but it is covered in thick clouds of sulfuric acid.

VENUS

MERCURY

SUN

MOON

EARTH

Where did Earth come from?

2 **The Earth came from a cloud in space.**
Scientists think it formed from a huge cloud
of gas and dust around 4,500 million years
ago. A star near the cloud exploded, making
the cloud spin. As the cloud spun, gases
gathered at its center and formed the Sun.
Dust whizzed around the Sun and began
to stick together to form lumps of rock. In
time, the rocks crashed into each other
and made the planets. The Earth is one
of these planets.

(5) The Earth was made up of one large piece of land, now split into seven chunks known as continents.

(1) Cloud starts to spin.

▶ Clouds of gas and dust are made from the remains of old stars that have exploded or run out of energy. It is from these clouds that new stars and planets form.

(4) Volcanoes erupt, releasing gases, helping to form the early atmosphere.

(3) The Earth begins to cool and a hard shell forms.

3 **At first the Earth was very
hot.** As the rocks collided they heated
each other up. Later, as the Earth
formed, the rocks inside it melted. The
new Earth was a ball of liquid rock with
a thin, solid shell.

(2) Dust gathers into lumps of rock that form a small planet.

4 Huge numbers of large rocks called meteorites crashed into the Earth. They made round hollows on the surface. These hollows are called craters. The Moon was hit with meteorites at the same time. Look at the Moon with binoculars—you can see the craters that were made long ago.

► The Moon was hit by meteorites, which made huge craters and mountain ranges up to 16,400 feet high.

▼ Erupting volcanoes and fierce storms helped form the atmosphere and oceans. These provided energy that was needed for life on Earth to begin.

5 The seas and oceans formed as the Earth cooled down. Volcanoes erupted, letting out steam, gases, and rocks. As the Earth cooled, the steam changed to water droplets and formed clouds. As the Earth cooled further, rain fell from the clouds. It took millions of years of rain to form the seas and oceans.

I DON'T BELIEVE IT!

Millions of rocks crash into Earth as it speeds through space. Some larger ones may reach the ground as meteorites.

In a spin

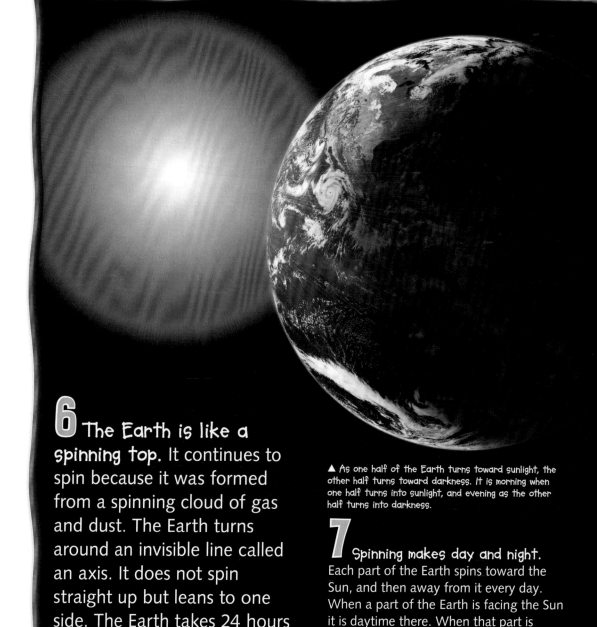

6 **The Earth is like a spinning top.** It continues to spin because it was formed from a spinning cloud of gas and dust. The Earth turns around an invisible line called an axis. It does not spin straight up but leans to one side. The Earth takes 24 hours to spin around once—we call this period of time a day.

▲ As one half of the Earth turns toward sunlight, the other half turns toward darkness. It is morning when one half turns into sunlight, and evening as the other half turns into darkness.

7 **Spinning makes day and night.** Each part of the Earth spins toward the Sun, and then away from it every day. When a part of the Earth is facing the Sun it is daytime there. When that part is facing away from the Sun it is nighttime. Is the Earth facing the Sun or facing away from it where you are?

8
The Earth spins around two points on its surface. They are at opposite ends of the planet. One is at the top of the Earth, called the North Pole. The other is at the bottom of the Earth. It is called the South Pole. The North and South Poles are covered by ice and snow all year round.

9
The spinning Earth acts like a magnet. At the center of the Earth is liquid iron. As the Earth spins, it makes the iron behave like a magnet with a North and South Pole. These act on the magnet in a compass to make the needle point to the North and South Poles.

North Pole

▼ If you were in space and looked at the Earth from the side, it would appear to move from left to right. If you looked down on Earth from the North Pole, it would seem to be moving counterclockwise.

Direction of Earth's spin

Axis

South Pole

▲ The region around the North Pole is called the Arctic. It consists of the Arctic Ocean, which is mainly covered in a layer of floating ice.

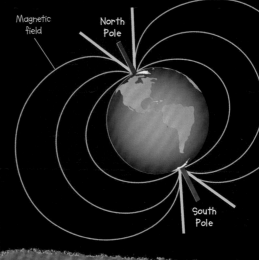

▼ These lines show the pulling power of the magnet inside the Earth.

Magnetic field

North Pole

South Pole

MAKE A COMPASS

You will need:
bowl of water   piece of wood
bar magnet   real compass

Place the wood in the water with the magnet on top. Make sure they do not touch the sides. When the wood is still, check which way the magnet is pointing with your compass, by placing it on a flat surface. It will tell you the direction of the Poles.

Inside the Earth

10 There are different layers inside the Earth. There is a thin, rocky crust on the surface, a solid middle called the mantle and a center called the core. The outer core is liquid but the inner part of the core is solid metal.

11 At the center of the Earth is a huge metal ball called the inner core. It is 1,500 miles wide and is made mainly from iron, with some nickel. The ball has an incredible temperature of around 12,000°F—hot enough to make the metals melt. However, they stay solid because the other layers of the Earth push down heavily on them.

12 Around the center of the Earth flows a hot, liquid layer of iron and nickel. This layer is the outer core and is about 1,300 miles thick. As the Earth spins, the inner and outer core move at different speeds.

13 The largest layer is called the mantle. It is around 1,800 miles thick. It lies between the core and the crust. The mantle is made of soft, hot rock. In the upper mantle, near the crust, the rock moves more slowly.

Crust

Atmosphere

Mantle 8,000°F

Outer core 9,000°F

Inner core 12,000°F

◀ The internal structure of the Earth. The center of the Earth—the inner core—is solid even though it is intensely hot. This is because it is under extreme pressure.

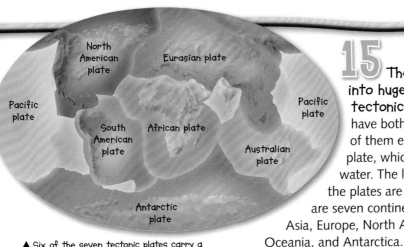

North
American
plate

Eurasian plate

Pacific
plate

Pacific
plate

South
American
plate

African plate

Australian
plate

Antarctic
plate

▲ Six of the seven tectonic plates carry a
continent. The Pacific plate does not.

15 The crust is divided into huge slabs of rock called tectonic plates. The plates all have both land and seas on top of them except for the Pacific plate, which is just covered by water. The large areas of land on the plates are called continents. There are seven continents in total—Africa, Asia, Europe, North America, South America, Oceania, and Antarctica.

14 The Earth's surface is covered by crust. Land is made of continental crust between 7.5 and 26 miles thick. Most of this is made from a rock called granite. The ocean bed is made of oceanic crust about three miles thick. It is made mainly from a rock called basalt.

▼ The Great Rift Valley in Kenya is part of a huge system of rift valleys. It is the result of tectonic plates moving apart, causing the Earth's crust to separate.

16 Very, very slowly, the continents are moving. Slow-flowing mantle under the crust moves the tectonic plates across the Earth's surface. As the plates move, so do the continents. In some places, the plates push into each other. In others, they move apart. North America is moving 2 inches away from Europe every year!

Hot rocks

17 **There are places on Earth where hot, liquid rocks shoot up through the surface.** These are volcanoes. Beneath a volcano is a huge space filled with molten (liquid) rock. This is the magma chamber. Inside the chamber, pressure builds like the pressure in a fizzy drink's can if you shake it. Ash, steam, and molten rock called lava escape from the top of the volcano—this is an eruption.

Lava flowing away from vent

Molten rock spreading out under the volcano and cooling down

Volcanic bomb

Shield volcano

Crater volcano

Cone-shaped volcano

▲ The three common types of volcano. Most volcanoes erupt along tectonic plate boundaries.

▶ When a volcano erupts, the hot rock from inside the Earth escapes as ash, smoke, lumps of rock called volcanic bombs, and rivers of lava.

18 **Volcanoes erupt in different ways and form different shapes.** Most have a central "pipe," reaching from the magma chamber up to the vent opening. Some volcanoes have runny lava. It flows from the vent and makes a domed shape called a shield volcano. Other volcanoes have thick lava. When they erupt, gases in the lava make it explode into pieces of ash. The ash settles on the lava to make a cone-shaped volcano. A caldera, or crater volcano, is made when the top of a cone-shaped volcano explodes and sinks into the magma chamber.

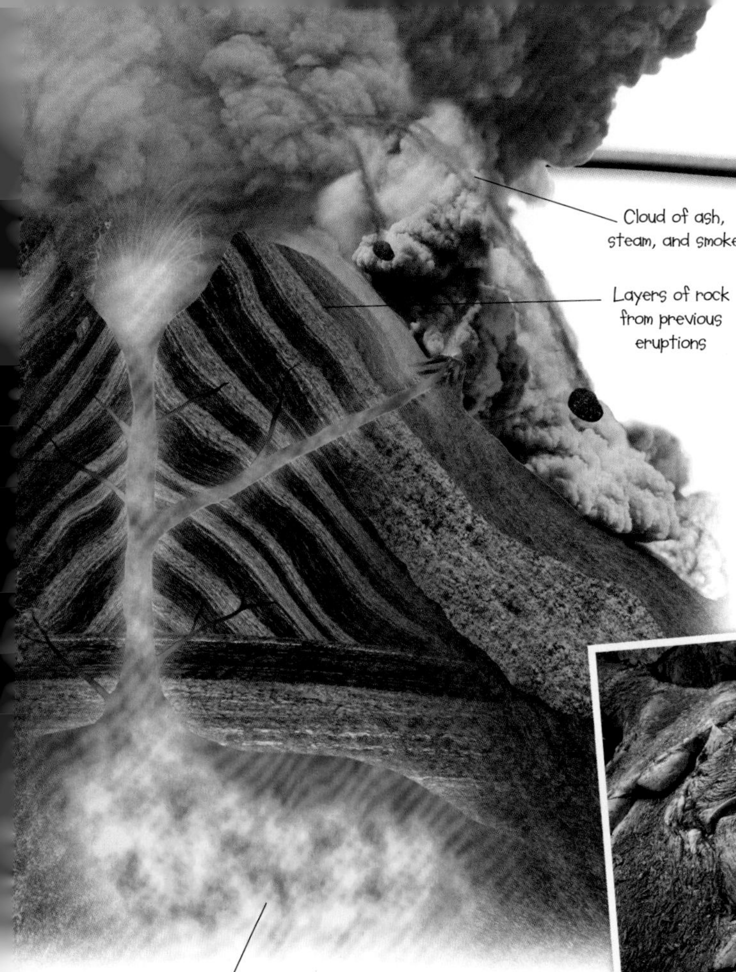

Cloud of ash, steam, and smoke

Layers of rock from previous eruptions

Huge chamber of magma (molten rock) beneath the volcano

▶ Pillow lava piles up on the coast of Hawaii, following an eruption of the Kilauea volcano.

19 There are volcanoes under the sea. Where tectonic plates move apart, lava flows out from rift volcanoes to fill the gap. The hot lava is cooled quickly by the sea and forms pillow-shaped lumps called pillow lava.

MAKE A VOLCANO

You will need:
baking soda   sand   a plastic bottle   vinegar   food coloring   gloves   covering for table

With help from an adult, put a tablespoon of baking soda in the bottle. Stand it in a tray with a cone of sand around it. Put a few drops of red food coloring in half a cup of vinegar. Pour this into the bottle. In a few moments the volcano should erupt with red, frothy lava.

20 Hot rocks don't always reach the surface. Huge lumps of rock can rise into the crust and become stuck. These are batholiths. The rock cools slowly and large crystals form. When the crystals cool, they form a rock called granite. In time, the surface of the crust may wear away and the top of the batholith appears above ground.

15

Boil and bubble

21 **Geysers can be found above old volcanoes.** If volcanoes collapse, the rocks settle above hot rocks in the magma chamber. The gaps between the broken rocks make pipes and chambers. Rain water collects in the chambers, where it heats until it boils. Steam builds up, pushing the water through the pipes and out of an opening called a nozzle. Steam and water shoot up, making a fountain up to 190 feet high.

MAKE A GEYSER

You will need:
bucket   plastic funnel   plastic tubing

Fill a bucket with water. Turn the plastic funnel upside down and sink most of it in the water. Take a piece of plastic tube and put one end under the funnel. Blow down the other end of the tube. A spray of water and air will shoot out of the funnel. Be prepared for a wet face!

22 **In a hot spring, the water bubbles gently to the surface.** As the water is heated in the chamber, it rises up a pipe and into a pool. The pool may be brightly colored due to tiny plants and animals called algae and bacteria. These live in large numbers in the hot water.

▶ In Iceland, visitors watch the Strokkur geyser erupt.

Clouds of mineral particles forming black smoke

Giant tube worms

Superheated water

Chimney (stack)

▲ The rocky chimneys of a black smoker are built up over time by minerals in the hot water.

24 **Wallowing in a mud pot can make your skin soft.** A mud pot is made when fumes from underground break down rocks into tiny pieces. These mix with water to make mud. Hot gases push through the mud, making it bubble. Some mud pots are cool enough to wallow in.

25 **Steam and smelly fumes can escape from holes in the ground.** These holes are called fumaroles. Since Roman times, people have used the steam from fumaroles for steam baths. The steam may keep joints and lungs healthy.

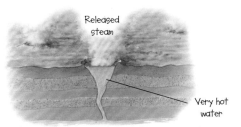

Released steam

Very hot water

▲ Under a fumarole the water gets so hot that it turns to steam, then shoots upward into the air.

23 **Deep in the ocean are hot springs called black smokers.** They form near rift volcanoes, where magma is close to the ocean floor. Water seeps into cracks in rocks and is heated. The hot water dissolves minerals from the surrounding rock as it travels upward. The minerals in the water produce dark clouds that look like smoke.

26 **In Iceland, underground steam is used to make lights work.** The steam is sent to power plants and is used to work generators to make electricity. The electricity then flows to homes and powers electrical equipment such as lights, televisions, and computers.

Breaking down rocks

27 **Ice has the power to break open rocks.** In cold weather, rain water gets into cracks in rocks and freezes. The water expands as it turns to ice. The ice pushes with such power on the rock that it opens up the cracks. Over a long time, a rock can be broken down into thousands of tiny pieces.

▲ Ice has broken through rocks in a creek, forcing the layers apart and breaking off fragments.

28 **Living things can break down rocks.** Sometimes a tree seed lands in a crack in a rock. In time, a tree grows and its large roots force open the rock. Tiny living things called lichens dissolve the surface of rocks to reach minerals they need to live. When animals, such as rabbits, make a burrow they may break up some of the rock in the ground.

▼ Tree roots grow in joints in many rocks. As the roots get larger, the rock is forced apart.

29 **Warming up and cooling down can break rocks into flakes.** When a rock warms up it swells a little. When it cools, the rock shrinks back to its original size. After swelling and shrinking many times, some rocks break up into flakes. Sometimes layers of large flakes form on a rock, making it look like the skin of an onion.

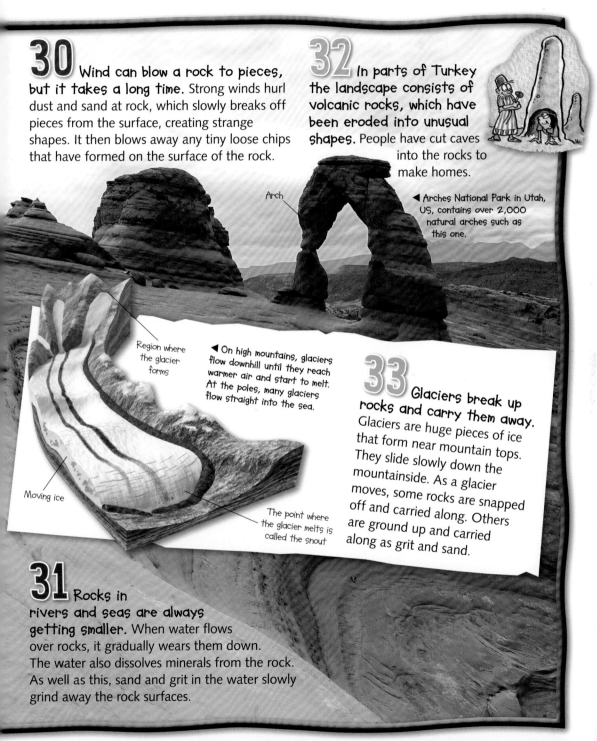

30 Wind can blow a rock to pieces, but it takes a long time. Strong winds hurl dust and sand at rock, which slowly breaks off pieces from the surface, creating strange shapes. It then blows away any tiny loose chips that have formed on the surface of the rock.

32 In parts of Turkey the landscape consists of volcanic rocks, which have been eroded into unusual shapes. People have cut caves into the rocks to make homes.

Arch

◀ Arches National Park in Utah, US, contains over 2,000 natural arches such as this one.

Region where the glacier forms

◀ On high mountains, glaciers flow downhill until they reach warmer air and start to melt. At the poles, many glaciers flow straight into the sea.

Moving ice

The point where the glacier melts is called the snout

33 Glaciers break up rocks and carry them away. Glaciers are huge pieces of ice that form near mountain tops. They slide slowly down the mountainside. As a glacier moves, some rocks are snapped off and carried along. Others are ground up and carried along as grit and sand.

31 Rocks in rivers and seas are always getting smaller. When water flows over rocks, it gradually wears them down. The water also dissolves minerals from the rock. As well as this, sand and grit in the water slowly grind away the rock surfaces.

Settling down

34 Stones of different sizes can combine to make rock. Thousands of years ago, boulders, pebbles, and gravel settled on the shores of seas and lakes. Over time, these have become stuck together to make a type of rock called conglomerate. At the foot of cliffs, broken, rocky pieces have collected and joined together to make a rock called breccia.

▲ Pieces of rock can become stuck together by a natural cement to make a lump of larger rock, such as breccia.

▼ These chalk cliffs in Dorset, England, have been eroded over time to create sea stacks.

35 A form of limestone, chalk is made from millions of shells of tiny sea creatures. A drop of sea water contains many microscopic organisms (living things), some of which have shells. When the organisms die, the shells sink to the seabed and in time form chalk, which builds up to form rocks and cliffs.

36
Limestone is basically the mineral calcite, often with bits from sea creatures, broken into various sizes. There are many types of limestone, depending on what it contains—shelly limestone has shells, coralline limestone has remains of corals, and so on.

▲ Limestone is usually white, cream, gray, or yellow. Caves often form in areas of limestone.

37
If mud is squashed hard enough, it turns to stone. Mud is made from tiny particles of clay and slightly larger particles called silt. When huge layers of mud formed in ancient rivers, lakes, and seas, they were squashed by their own weight to make mudstone.

▶ Mudstone has a very smooth surface. It may be gray, black, brown, or yellow.

38
Sandstone can be made in the sea or in the desert. When a thick layer of sand builds up, the grains are pressed together and cement forms. This sticks the grains together to make sandstone. Sea sandstone may be yellow with sharp-edged grains. Desert sandstone may be red with round, smooth grains.

◀ Sandstone can form impressive shapes. These pillars in Arches National Park, Utah, US, are known as the Fins.

I DON'T BELIEVE IT!
Flint is found in chalk and limestone. Thousands of years ago people used flint to make axes, knives, and arrow heads.

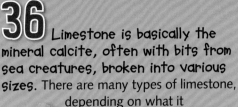

Uncovering fossils

39 Fossils are formed from animals and plants that were buried. When a plant or animal dies, it is usually eaten by other living things so that nothing remains. If the plant or animal was buried quickly after death, or even buried alive, its body may be preserved.

▼ Prehistoric ocean-dwelling creatures, such as this ichthyosaur, are more likely to leave fossils than those on land.

① The ichthyosaur lives on the ocean floor.

② After death, the ichthyosaur sinks to the seabed. Worms, crabs, and other scavengers eat its soft body parts.

③ Sediments cover the hard body parts, such as bones and teeth, which gradually turn into solid rock.

④ Millions of years later the upper rock layers wear away and the fossilized remains are exposed.

40 A fossil is made from minerals. A dead plant or animal can be dissolved by water. An empty space in the shape of the plant or animal is left in the mud and fills with minerals from the surrounding rock.

41 The first living things were probably single cells like today's bacteria and blue-green algae. Some fossils of bacteria are three and a half billion years old.

42 Some fossils look like coiled snakes, but are really shellfish. These are called ammonites. The ammonite's body was covered by a spiral shell. When it died, the body rotted away leaving the shell to become the fossil. Ammonites lived in the seas from 400–65 million years ago.

▶ When this ammonite was alive, tentacles would have stuck out from the uncoiled end of the shell.

44 Electricity in your home may have been made by burning fossils. About 300 million years ago the land was covered by forests and swamps. When plants died they fell into the swamps and did not rot away. Over time, their remains were compressed and heated so much that they turned to coal. Today, coal is used to work generators that make electricity.

▲ It is very rare to find complete fossil skeletons like this.

43 Whole skeletons of some dinosaurs have been found. But most dinosaurs left behind only a few fossilized bones. Fossilized teeth, skin, eggs, and droppings have also been discovered. When dinosaurs walked across mud they left tracks behind that became fossils. By looking at these, scientists have discovered how dinosaurs moved and how fast they could run.

Rocks that change

45 When a rock forms in the Earth's crust it may soon be changed again. There are two main ways this can happen. The rock is heated by hot rocks moving up through the crust, or the crust is squashed and heated as mountains form. Both of these ways make crystals in rock change to form new types of rocks, called metamorphic rock.

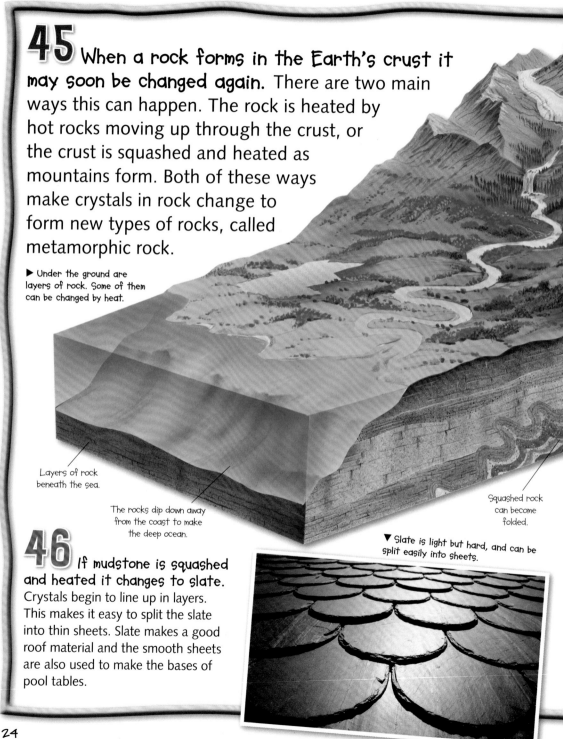

▶ Under the ground are layers of rock. Some of them can be changed by heat.

Layers of rock beneath the sea.

The rocks dip down away from the coast to make the deep ocean.

Squashed rock can become folded.

▼ Slate is light but hard, and can be split easily into sheets.

46 If mudstone is squashed and heated it changes to slate. Crystals begin to line up in layers. This makes it easy to split the slate into thin sheets. Slate makes a good roof material and the smooth sheets are also used to make the bases of pool tables.

48 Rock can become stripy when it is heated and folded. It becomes so hot, it almost melts. Minerals that make up the rock form layers that appear as colored stripes. These stripes may be wavy, showing the way the rock has been folded. This type of rock is called gneiss (sounds like "nice"). Gneiss that is billions of years old has been found under volcanoes in Canada.

Some hot rock travels to the surface through the pipe in a volcano.

Layers of rock away from the heat remain unchanged.

Hot rock trapped in the crust can change the rock around it.

▼ The stripes in gneiss are formed by layers of different minerals.

▼ Marble is often used to make ornaments like this Egyptian-style cat.

47 If limestone is heated in the Earth's crust it turns to marble. The shells that make up limestone break up when they are heated strongly and form marble, a rock that has a sugary appearance. The surface of marble can be polished to make it look attractive, and it is used to make statues and ornaments.

QUIZ

1. If a sandstone has red, round, smooth grains, where was the sand made?
2. Which rocks are made from seashells and tiny sea creatures?
3. Name six kinds of dinosaur fossil.
4. Which rock changes into slate?

Answers:
1. The desert 2. Limestone and chalk 3. Bones, teeth, skin, eggs, droppings, tracks 4. Mudstone

Massive mountains

49 The youngest mountains are the highest. Young mountains have jagged peaks because softer rocks on the top are broken down by weather. The peaks are made from harder rocks that take longer to break down. In time, even these hard rocks are worn away. This makes an older mountain shorter and gives its top a rounded shape.

▶ It takes millions of years for mountains to form, and the process is happening all the time. A group of mountains is called a range. The biggest ranges are the Alps in Europe, the Andes in South America, the Rockies in North America, and the highest of all—the Himalayas in Asia.

50 When plates in the Earth's crust collide, mountains are formed. When two continental plates push into each other, the crust at the edge of the plates crumples and folds, pushing up mountain ranges. The Himalayan Mountains in Asia formed in this way.

▼ The Himalayan range contains some of the world's highest mountains, including Mount Everest, the highest of all at 29,030 feet.

Mountain range is pushed up

Folded and uplifted rock

Fold mountain

51 Some of the Earth's highest mountains are volcanoes. These are formed when molten rock (lava) erupts through the Earth's crust. As the lava cools, it forms a rocky layer. With each new eruption, another layer is added.

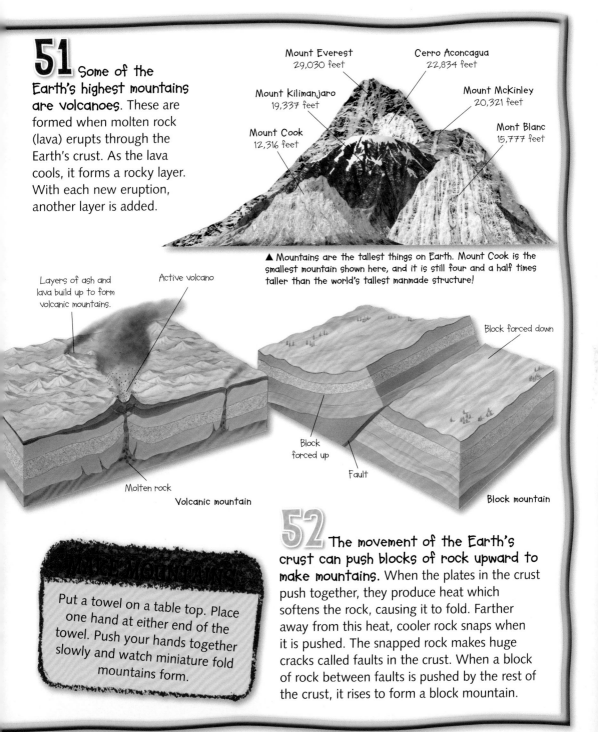

Mount Everest 29,030 feet

Cerro Aconcagua 22,834 feet

Mount Kilimanjaro 19,337 feet

Mount Mckinley 20,321 feet

Mount Cook 12,316 feet

Mont Blanc 15,777 feet

▲ Mountains are the tallest things on Earth. Mount Cook is the smallest mountain shown here, and it is still four and a half times taller than the world's tallest manmade structure!

Layers of ash and lava build up to form volcanic mountains.

Active volcano

Block forced down

Molten rock

Volcanic mountain

Block forced up

Fault

Block mountain

MAKE MOUNTAINS

Put a towel on a table top. Place one hand at either end of the towel. Push your hands together slowly and watch miniature fold mountains form.

52 The movement of the Earth's crust can push blocks of rock upward to make mountains. When the plates in the crust push together, they produce heat which softens the rock, causing it to fold. Farther away from this heat, cooler rock snaps when it is pushed. The snapped rock makes huge cracks called faults in the crust. When a block of rock between faults is pushed by the rest of the crust, it rises to form a block mountain.

Shaking the Earth

53 An earthquake is caused by violent movements in the Earth's crust. Most occur when two plates in the crust move against each other. An earthquake starts deep underground at its "focus." Shock waves move out in all directions, shaking the rock. The point where the shock waves reach the surface is called the epicenter. This is where the strongest shaking takes place.

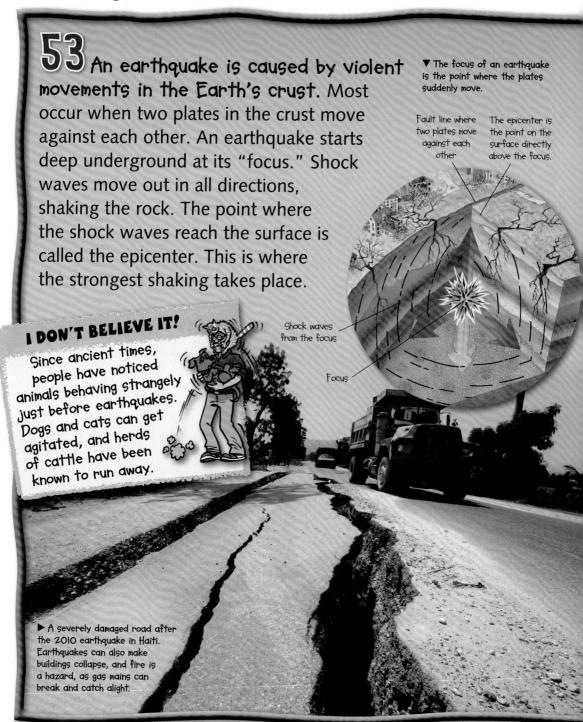

▼ The focus of an earthquake is the point where the plates suddenly move.

Fault line where two plates move against each other

The epicenter is the point on the surface directly above the focus.

Shock waves from the focus

Focus

I DON'T BELIEVE IT!

Since ancient times, people have noticed animals behaving strangely just before earthquakes. Dogs and cats can get agitated, and herds of cattle have been known to run away.

▶ A severely damaged road after the 2010 earthquake in Haiti. Earthquakes can also make buildings collapse, and fire is a hazard, as gas mains can break and catch alight.

54

The power of an earthquake can vary. Half a million earthquakes happen every year but hardly any of these can be felt. About 25 earthquakes each year are powerful enough to cause disasters. Earthquake strength is measured by the Richter Scale. The higher the number on the scale, the more destructive the earthquake.

▼ The Richter Scale measures the strength of the shock waves and energy produced by an earthquake. The shock waves can have little effect, or be strong enough to topple buildings.

Windows break at level 5

Bridges and buildings collapse at level 7

Widespread destruction occurs at level 8

As the tall tsunami reaches shallow water, it surges forward onto the shore.

Decreasing depth slows speed but increases wave height.

Upward wave

An earthquake beneath the sea floor causes a sudden movement of a massive column of water.

55

Earthquakes under the sea are called seaquakes. These can cause enormous, devastating waves called tsunamis. As the tsunami rushes across the ocean, it stays quite low. As it reaches the coast, it slows and the water piles up to form a wall. The wave rushes onto the land, destroying everything in its path.

◄ A tsunami can be up to 100 feet high. The weight and power in the wave flattens towns and villages in its path.

Cavernous caves

56 When rain falls on limestone it becomes a cave-maker. Rain water can mix with carbon dioxide to form an acid strong enough to attack limestone and make it dissolve. Underground, the action of the rain water makes caves in which streams, waterfalls, and lakes can be found.

▼ Rain water flows through the cracks in limestone and makes them wider to eventually form caves. The horizontal caves are called galleries and the vertical caves are called shafts.

Waterfall in a shaft

Gallery

Cave opening

57

Some caves are made from tubes of lava. As lava moves down the side of a volcano, its surface cools down quickly. The cold lava becomes solid but below, the lava remains warm and keeps flowing. Under the solid surface a tube may form in which liquid lava flows. When the tube empties, a cave is formed.

▶ This cave made by lava in Hawaii is so large that people can walk through it without having to bend down.

58

Dripping water in a limestone cave makes rock spikes. When water drips from a cave roof it leaves a small amount of limestone behind. A spike of rock begins to form. This rock spike, called a stalactite, grows from the ceiling. Where the drops splash onto the cave floor, tiny pieces of limestone gather. They form a spike which points upward. This is a stalagmite.

59

The longest stalactite is 193 feet long. The tallest stalagmite is 104 feet tall. Over long periods of time, a stalactite and a stalagmite may join together to form a column of rock.

▼ Carlsbad Caverns in New Mexico, US, are famous for limestone rock formations such as stalactites and stalagmites.

STALACTITES

STALAGMITES

The Earth's treasure

60 Gold can form small grains, large nuggets, or veins in rocks. When the rocks wear away, the gold may be found in the sand of river beds. Silver forms branching wires in rock. It does not shine like silver jewelry, but is covered in a black coating called tarnish.

◀ Aluminum must be extracted from its ore—bauxite (shown here)—before it can be used to make all kinds of things, from kitchen foil to airplanes.

61 Most metals are found in rocks called ores. An ore is a mixture of different substances, of which metal is one. Each metal has its own ore. For example, aluminum is found in an ore called bauxite. Heat is used to extract metals from their ores. We use metals to make thousands of different things, ranging from watches to jumbo jets.

62 Beautiful crystals can grow in lava bubbles. Lava contains gases which form bubbles. When the lava cools and becomes solid, the bubbles create balloon-shaped spaces in the rock. These are called geodes. Liquids seep into them and form large crystals. The gemstone amethyst forms in this way.

▲ A woman pans for gold in the Mekong River in Southeast Asia.

▲ Inside a geode there is space for crystals to spread out, grow and form perfect shapes.

January
Garnet

February
Amethyst

March
Aquamarine

April
Diamond

May
Emerald

June
Pearl

July
Ruby

August
Peridot

September
Sapphire

October
Opal

63 Gemstones are colored rocks that are cut and polished to make them sparkle. People have used them to make jewelry for thousands of years. Gems such as topaz, emerald, and garnet formed in hot rocks that rose to the Earth's crust and cooled. Most are found as small crystals, but a gem called beryl can have a huge crystal—the largest ever found was 60 feet long! Diamond is a gemstone and is the hardest natural substance found on Earth.

▲ There are more than 100 different kinds of gemstone. Some are associated with different months of the year and are known as "birthstones." For example, the birthstone for September is sapphire.

November
Topaz

December
Turquoise

MAKE SALT CRYSTALS

You will need:
table salt
magnifying glass
dark-colored bowl

Dissolve some table salt in some warm water. Pour the salty water into a dark-colored bowl. Put the bowl in a warm place so the water can evaporate. After a few days, you can look at the crystals with a magnifying glass.

Lands of sand and grass

64 The driest places on Earth are deserts. In many deserts there is a short period of rain each year, but some deserts have completely dry weather for many years. The main deserts of the world are shown on the map.

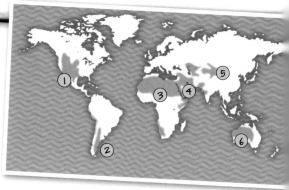

▲ This map shows the major deserts of the world.
① North American deserts—Great Basin and Mojave
② Atacama ③ Sahara ④ Arabian ⑤ Gobi ⑥ Australian deserts—Great Sandy, Gibson, Great Victoria, Simpson.

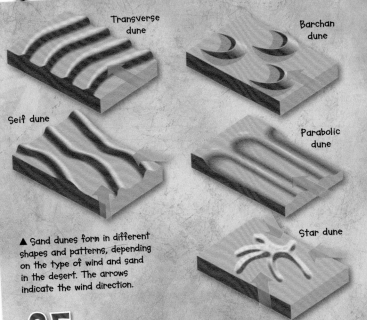

Transverse dune

Seif dune

Barchan dune

Parabolic dune

Star dune

▲ Sand dunes form in different shapes and patterns, depending on the type of wind and sand in the desert. The arrows indicate the wind direction.

66 Deserts are not always hot. It can be as hot as 122°F in the day, but at night the temperature falls as there are less clouds to trap in heat. Deserts near the Equator have hot days all year round, but some deserts farther away have very cold winters.

67 Camels are adapted for desert life. Fat deposits in their humps allow them to live without water for months, and their broad feet stop them from sinking into hot sand.

65 Sand dunes are made by winds blowing across a desert. If there is only a small amount of loose sand on the desert floor, the wind creates crescent-shaped dunes called barchans. If there is plenty of sand, it forms long, straight dunes called transverse dunes. If the wind blows in two directions, it makes long wavy dunes called seif dunes.

▲ Plants and animals can thrive at an oasis in the middle of a desert.

70 Grasslands are found in areas where there is more rain than a desert. They are open spaces where trees rarely grow. Tropical grasslands near the Equator are hot all year round. Grasslands farther away have warm summers and cool winters.

71 Large numbers of animals live on grasslands. In Africa, zebras feed on the top of grass stalks, while gnus eat the middle leaves and gazelles feed on the new shoots. This allows all the animals to feed together. Other animals such as lions feed on the plant-eaters.

68 An oasis is a pool of water in the desert. It forms from rain water that has seeped into the sand and collected in rocks beneath. The water moves through the rock to where the sand is very thin and forms a pool. Trees and plants grow around the pool and animals visit it to drink.

69 A desert cactus stores water in its stem. The grooves on the stem let it swell with water to keep it alive in the dry weather. The spines stop animals biting into the cactus for a drink.

▶ Different animals can live together by eating grass at differing levels. Zebras ① eat the tall grass. Gnus ② eat the middle shoots and gazelles ③ graze on the lowest shoots.

Fantastic forests

72 There are three main kinds of forest. They are coniferous, temperate, and tropical forests. Each grow in different regions of the world, depending on the climate.

▲ This map shows the major areas of forest in the world:

① Coniferous forest
② Temperate forest
③ Tropical forest

73 Coniferous trees form huge forests around the northern part of the planet. They have long, green, needlelike leaves covered in a waxy coating. These trees stay in leaf throughout the year. In winter, the waxy surface helps snow slide off the leaves so that sunlight can reach them to keep them alive. Coniferous trees produce seeds in cones.

◀ Squirrels can open seed cones from coniferous trees in just a few seconds.

74 Most trees in temperate forests have flat, broad leaves and need large amounts of water to keep them alive. In winter, the trees cannot get enough water from the frozen ground, so they lose their leaves and grow new ones in spring. Deer, rabbits, foxes, and mice live on the woodland floor while squirrels, woodpeckers, and owls live in the trees.

▲ A jaguar stalks through a dense tropical forest in Belize.

▲ The Hoh temperate rain forest in Washington state, US, is home to elks, bears, and cougars.

75 Large numbers of trees grow close together in a tropical forest. They have broad, evergreen leaves and branches that almost touch. These form a leafy roof over the forest called a canopy. It rains almost every day in a tropical rain forest. The vegetation is so thick, it can take a raindrop ten minutes to reach the ground. Three-quarters of all known animal and plant species live in rain forests. They include huge spiders, brightly colored frogs, and jungle cats.

1. What forms at the top of a cloud?
2. What shape is a barchan sand dune?
3. In which kind of forest would you find brightly colored frogs?

Answers:
1. Snowflakes 2. Crescent
3. Tropical rain forest

Rivers and lakes

76 **A river can start from a spring.** This is where water flows from the ground. Rain soaks through the ground, and gushes out from the side of a hill. The trickle of water that flows from a spring is called a stream. Many streams join to make a river.

77 **A river changes as it flows to the sea.** Rivers begin in hills and mountains. They are narrow and flow quickly there. When the river flows through flatter land it becomes wider and slow-moving. It makes loops called meanders that may separate and form oxbow lakes. The point where the river meets the sea is the river mouth. This may be a wide channel called an estuary or a group of sandy islands called a delta.

◀ Waterfalls may only be a few inches high, or come crashing over a cliff with a massive drop. Angel Falls in Venezuela form the highest falls in the world. One of the drops is an amazing 2,648 feet.

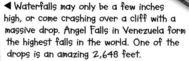

78 **Water wears rocks down to make a waterfall.** When a river flows from a layer of hard rock onto softer rock, it wears the softer rock down. The rocks and pebbles in the water grind the soft rock away to make a cliff face. At the bottom of the waterfall they make a deep pool called a plunge pool.

KEY

1. Headwater
2. Meander
3. Oxbow lake
4. River mouth (delta)

◀ High in the mountains, streams join to form the headwater of a river. From here the river flows through the mountains, then more slowly across the plains to the sea.

80 Lakes often form in hollows in the ground. The hollows may be left when glaciers melt or plates in the Earth's crust move apart. Some lakes form when a landslide makes a dam across a river.

▲ A landslide has fallen into the river and blocked the flow of water to make a lake.

81 A lake can form in the crater of a volcano. A few have also formed in craters left by meteorites that hit Earth long ago.

▼ This lake was formed in a volcanic crater.

◀ Most lakes are blue, but some are green, pink, red, or even white. The Laguna Colorado in Chile is red due to tiny organisms (creatures) that live in the water.

79 Some lake water can be brightly colored. The colors are made by tiny organisms called algae or by minerals dissolved in the water.

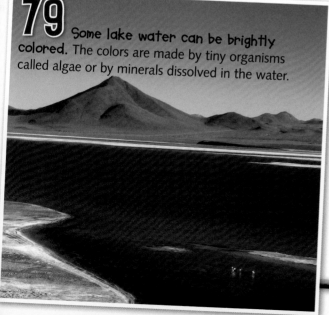

World of water

82 There is so much water on our planet that it could be called "Ocean" instead of Earth. Only about one third of the planet is covered by land. The rest is covered by five huge areas of water called oceans. A sea is a smaller area of water within an ocean. For example, the North Sea is part of the Atlantic Ocean and the Malayan Sea is part of the Pacific Ocean.

83 Coasts are always changing. The point where the sea and land meet is called the coast (1). In many places waves crash onto the land and erode it. Caves (2) and arches (3) are punched into cliffs. In time, the arches break and leave columns of rock called sea stacks (4).

◀ The action of the waves gradually erodes the coastline to create different features.

Continental shelf   Continental slope

84 The oceans are so deep that mountains are hidden beneath them. If you paddle by the shore the water is quite shallow, but at its deepest point, the ocean reaches 35,797 feet. The ocean floor is a flat plain with mountain ranges rising across it. These mark where two tectonic plates meet. Nearer the coast are deep trenches where the edges of two plates have moved apart. Extinct volcanoes form mountains called seamounts.

▼ Corals only grow in tropical or subtropical waters. They tend to grow in shallow water where there is lots of sunlight.

85 **Tiny creatures can make islands in the oceans.** Coral is made from the leftover skeletons of sea creatures called polyps. Over millions of years the skeletons build up to form huge coral reefs. Coral also builds up to create islands around extinct volcanoes in the Pacific and Indian Oceans.

86 **There are thousands of icebergs floating in the oceans.** They are made from glaciers and ice sheets which have formed at the North and South Poles. Only about a tenth of an iceberg can be seen above water. The rest lies below and can damage and sink ships that sail too close.

▶ Under every iceberg is a huge amount of ice, usually much bigger than the area visible from the surface.

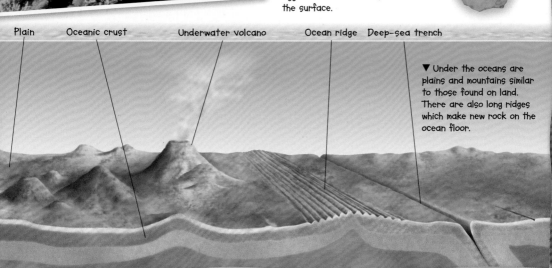

Plain   Oceanic crust   Underwater volcano   Ocean ridge   Deep-sea trench

▼ Under the oceans are plains and mountains similar to those found on land. There are also long ridges which make new rock on the ocean floor.

41

The planet of life

87 **There are millions of different kinds of life forms on Earth.** So far, life has not been found anywhere else. Living things survive here because it is warm, there is water, and the air contains oxygen. If we discover other planets with these conditions, there may be life on them too.

▼ Despite being the biggest fish in the oceans, the mighty whale shark feeds on tiny shrimplike creatures.

88 **The star-nosed mole has feelers on the end of its nose.** It uses them to find food.

▼ This caterpillar eats as much plant life as possible before beginning its change to a butterfly.

89 **Many living things on the Earth are tiny.** They are so small that we cannot see them. A whale shark is the largest fish on the planet, yet it feeds on tiny shrimplike creatures. These in turn feed on even smaller plantlike organisms called plankton, which make food from sunlight and sea water. Microscopic bacteria are found in the soil and even on your skin.

90 **Animals cannot live without plants.** A plant makes food from sunlight, water, air, and minerals in the soil. Animals cannot make their own food so many of them eat plants. Others survive by eating the plant-eaters. If plants died out, all the animals would die too.

91 The air can be full of animals. On a warm day, clouds of midges and gnats form close to the ground. In spring and fall, flocks of birds fly to different parts of the world to nest. On summer evenings bats hunt for midges flying in the air.

92 The surface of the ground is home to many small animals. Mice scurry through the grass. Larger animals such as deer hide in bushes. The elephant is the largest land animal. It does not need to hide because few animals would attack it.

93 If you dig into the ground you can find animals living there. The earthworm is a common creature found in the soil. It feeds on rotting plants that it pulls into the soil. Earthworms are eaten by moles that dig their way underground.

▲ Animals thrive in many different kinds of habitats on Earth. The skies, the ground, and even underground are home to countless forms of life.

ATLANTIC OCEAN

PACIFIC OCEAN

94 Oceans cover more than two thirds of the Earth's rocky surface. Their total area is about 140 million square miles, which means there is more than twice as much ocean as land! Although all the oceans flow into each other, we know them as five different oceans—the Pacific, Atlantic, Indian, Southern, and Arctic. Our landmasses, the continents, rise out of the oceans.

95 The largest, deepest ocean is the Pacific. It covers nearly half of our planet and is double the size of the Atlantic, the next largest ocean. In places, the Pacific is so deep that the Earth's tallest mountain, Everest, would sink without a trace.

▼ The point where the ocean meets the land is called the seashore.

96 Oceans can look blue, green, or gray. This is because of the way light hits the surface. Water soaks up the red parts of light, but scatters the blue-green parts, making the sea look different shades of blue or green.

ARCTIC OCEAN

INDIAN OCEAN

SOUTHERN OCEAN

▲ Less than 10 percent of the world's oceans have been explored.

97 Seas can be red or dead. A sea is a small part of an ocean. The Red Sea, for example, is the part of the Indian Ocean between Egypt and Saudi Arabia. Asia's Dead Sea gets its name because it is so salty that living things can't survive there.

98 There are streams in the oceans. All the water in the oceans is constantly moving, but in some places it flows as currents, which take particular paths. One of these is the warm Gulf Stream, that travels around the edge of the Atlantic Ocean.

I DON'T BELIEVE IT!

Oceans hold 97 percent of the world's water. Just a fraction is in freshwater lakes and rivers.

Ocean features

99 There are plains, mountains, and valleys under the oceans, in areas called basins. Each basin has a rim (the flat continental shelf that meets the shore) and sides (the continental slope that drops away from the shelf). In the ocean basin there are flat abyssal plains, steep hills, huge underwater volcanoes called seamounts, and deep valleys called trenches.

Continental slope

Land

Continental shelf

Spreading ridge

Abyssal trench

Abyssal hills

▲ Under the oceans there is a landscape similar to that found on land.

▼ As the magma (molten rock) cools, the ocean floor spreads out.

Spreading floor

Ridge

Magma

100 The ocean floor is spreading. Molten (liquid) rock inside the Earth seeps from holes on the seabed. As the rock cools, it forms new sections of floor that creep slowly out. Scientists have proved this fact by looking at layers of rock on the ocean floor. There are matching stripes of rock either side of a ridge. Each pair came from the same hot rock eruption, then slowly spread out.

Seamount

Volcanic island

Ocean trench

101
Some islands are swallowed by the ocean. Sometimes, a ring-shaped coral reef called an atoll marks where a volcanic island once was. The coral reef built up around the island. After the volcano sank underwater, the reef remained.

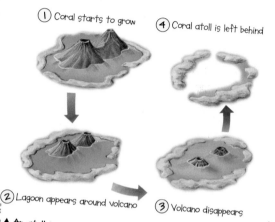

① Coral starts to grow

④ Coral atoll is left behind

② Lagoon appears around volcano

③ Volcano disappears

▲ An atoll is a ring-shaped coral reef that encloses a deep lagoon. It is left when an island sinks underwater.

102
New islands are born all the time. When an underwater volcano erupts, its lava cools in the water. Layers of lava build up, and the volcano grows in size. Eventually, it is tall enough to peep above the waves. The Hawaiian islands rose from the sea like this.

I DON'T BELIEVE IT!

The world's longest mountain chain is under the ocean. It is the Mid-Ocean range and stretches around the middle of the Earth.

▶ The Hawaiian islands were built up from layers of lava. There are still more to come.

Tides and shores

103
The sea level rises and falls twice each day along the coast. This is known as high and low tides. Tides happen because of the pull of the Moon's gravity, which lifts water from the part of Earth's surface facing it.

▼ At high tide, the sea rises up the shore and dumps seaweed, shells, and driftwood. Most coasts have two high tides and two low tides every day.

High tides happen at the same time each day on opposite sides of the Earth.

At high tide the water level rises.

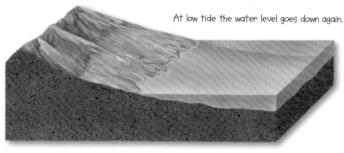

At low tide the water level goes down again.

104
Spring tides are especially high. They occur twice a month, when the Moon is in line with the Earth and the Sun. Then, the Sun's pulling force joins the Moon's and seawater is lifted higher than usual. The opposite happens when the Moon and Sun are at right angles to each other. Then, their pulling powers work against each other causing weak neap tides —the lowest high tides and low tides.

▶ Spring tides occur when the Sun and the Moon are lined up and pulling together.

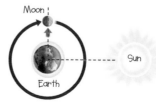

◀ Neap tides occur when the Sun and Moon are at right angles to each other and pulling in different directions.

105
The sea is strong enough to carve into rock. Pounding waves batter coastlines and erode, or wear away, the rock.

▼ Erosion can create amazing shapes such as arches, and pillars called sea stacks.

Sea stack

Arch

107
Sand is found on bars and spits, as well as beaches. It is made up of grains of worn-down rock and shell. Sand collects on shorelines and spits, but also forms on offshore beaches called sand bars. Spits are narrow ridges of worn sand and pebbles.

108
Some shores are swampy. This makes the border between land and sea hard to pinpoint. Muddy coastlines include tropical mangrove swamps that are flooded by salty water from the sea.

▶ The stilt roots of mangrove trees can take in nutrients from the water.

The biggest tsunami was taller than five Statues of Liberty! It hit the Japanese Ryuku Islands in 1771.

106
Tsunamis are the most powerful waves. They happen when underwater earthquakes trigger tremendous shock waves. These whip up a wall of water that travels across the ocean's surface.

Life in a rock pool

109 Rock pools are teeming with all kinds of creatures. Limpets are a kind of shellfish. They live on rocks and in pools at shorelines. Here, they eat slimy, green algae, but they have to withstand the crashing tide. They cling to the rock with their muscular foot, only moving when the tide is out.

110 Some anemones fight with harpoons. Beadlet anemones will sometimes fight over a feeding ground. Their weapon is the poison they usually use to stun their prey. They shoot tiny hooks like harpoons at each other until the weakest one gives in.

▶ Anemones are named after flowers, because their arms are like petals.

▶ Starfish are relatives of brittle stars, sea urchins, and sea cucumbers.

111 Starfish can grow new arms. They may have as many as 40 arms, or rays. If a predator grabs hold of one, the starfish abandons the ray, and uses the others to make its getaway!

50

112

Hermit crabs do not have shells. Most crabs shed their shells as they outgrow them, but the hermit crab does not have a shell. It borrows the leftover shell of a dead whelk or other mollusk—whatever it can squeeze into to protect its soft body. These crabs have even been spotted using a coconut shell as a home!

▶ Hermit crabs protect their soft bodies in a borrowed shell.

113

Sea urchins wear a disguise. Green sea urchins sometimes drape themselves with bits of shell, pebble, and seaweed. This makes the urchin more difficult for predators, or hunters, to spot.

114

Sponges are animals! They are very simple creatures that filter food from seawater. The natural sponge that you might use in the bath is a long-dead, dried-out sponge.

◀ There are about 4,500 different types of sponge in the sea.

Colorful coral

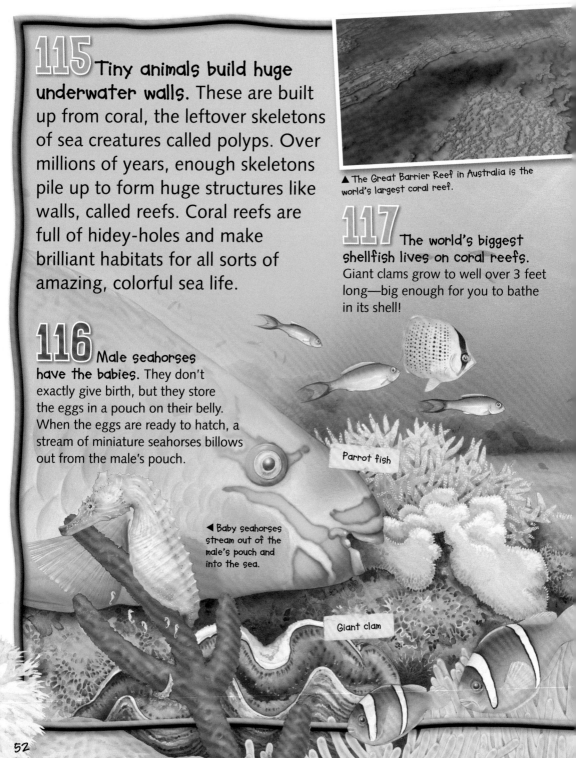

115 **Tiny animals build huge underwater walls.** These are built up from coral, the leftover skeletons of sea creatures called polyps. Over millions of years, enough skeletons pile up to form huge structures like walls, called reefs. Coral reefs are full of hidey-holes and make brilliant habitats for all sorts of amazing, colorful sea life.

▲ The Great Barrier Reef in Australia is the world's largest coral reef.

117 **The world's biggest shellfish lives on coral reefs.** Giant clams grow to well over 3 feet long—big enough for you to bathe in its shell!

116 **Male seahorses have the babies.** They don't exactly give birth, but they store the eggs in a pouch on their belly. When the eggs are ready to hatch, a stream of miniature seahorses billows out from the male's pouch.

◀ Baby seahorses stream out of the male's pouch and into the sea.

Parrot fish

Giant clam

118 Some fish go to the cleaners. Cleaner wrasse are little fish that are paid for cleaning! Larger fish, such as groupers and moray eels visit the wrasse, which eat all the parasites and other bits of dirt off the bigger fishes' bodies—what a feast!

119 Clownfish are sting-proof. Most creatures steer clear of an anemone's stinging tentacles. But the clownfish swims among the stingers, where it's safe from predators. Strangely, the anemone doesn't seem to sting the clownfish.

120 Some fish look like stones. Stonefish rest on the seabed, looking just like the rocks that surround them. If they are spotted, the poisonous spines on their backs can stun an attacker in seconds.

I DON'T BELIEVE IT!
You can see the Great Barrier Reef from space! At over 1,200 miles long, it is the largest structure ever built by living creatures.

Lion fish

Cleaner wrasse fish

Stonefish

Clownfish

▲ Tropical coral reefs are the habitat of an amazing range of marine plants and creatures.

Swimming machines

121 **There are over 21,000 different types of fish in the sea.** They range from huge whale sharks to tiny gobies. Almost all are covered in scales and use fins and a muscular tail to power through the water. Like their freshwater cousins, sea fish have slits called gills that take oxygen from the water so they can breathe.

▶ In a large group called a school, fish like these yellow snappers have less chance of being picked off by a predator.

122 **The oarfish is bigger than an oar—it can be as long as four canoes!** It is the longest bony fish and is found in all the world's oceans. Oarfish are striking creatures—they have a red fin along the length of their back.

◀ People once thought oarfish swam horizontally through the water. Now they know they swim upright.

123 **Sunfish like sunbathing!** Ocean sunfish are very large, broad fish that can weigh up to one ton. They are named after their habit of sunbathing on the surface of the ocean.

◀ At over 10 feet long, sunfish are the biggest bony fish in the oceans. They feed on plankton.

124 Flying fish cannot really fly. Fish can't survive out of water, but flying fish sometimes leap above the waves when they are traveling at high speeds. They use their winglike fins to keep them in the air for as long as 30 seconds.

▲ Flying fish feed near the surface so they are easy to find. Their gliding flight helps them escape most hunters.

125 Not all fish are the same shape. Cod or mackerel are what we think of as a normal fish shape, but fish come in all shapes and sizes. Flounder and other flatfish have squashed-flat bodies. Eels are so long and thin that the biggest types look like snakes, while tiny garden eels resemble worms! And of course, seahorses and seadragons look nothing like other fish at all!

▶ The flounder's flattened shape and dull coloring help to camouflage (hide) it on the seabed.

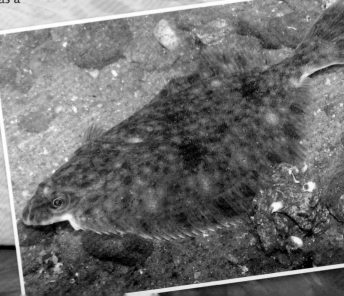

Shark!

▼ Great white sharks are fierce hunters. They will attack and eat almost anything, but prefer to feed on seals.

126 Great whites are the scariest sharks in the oceans. These powerful predators have been known to kill people and can speed through the water at 18 miles per hour. Unlike most fish, the great white is warm-blooded. This allows its muscles to work well, but also means the shark has to feed on plenty of meat.

▶ Basking sharks eat enormous amounts of plankton, which they sieve from the water as they swim.

127 Most sharks are meat-eaters. Herring are a favorite food for sand tiger and thresher sharks, while a tiger shark will eat just about anything! Strangely, some of the biggest sharks take the smallest prey. Whale sharks and basking sharks eat tiny sea creatures called plankton.

I DON'T BELIEVE IT!

Some sharks, such as dogfish and zebra sharks, don't look after their pups. They leave them to fend for themselves.

128 Sharks are shaped like torpedos.

Most sharks are built for speed, with a long streamlined body. This means water can move past them easily. A shark's fins keep it the right way up in the water, and help it to change direction quickly, so it can chase its prey. Sharks also have special cells in their heads, called ampullae of Lorenzini. These allow them to sense electricity given out by nearby fish.

Nostril

Dorsal fin

Jaw

Ampullae of Lorenzini

▶ The different features of a shark's body help it to be a successful hunter.

Gill

Pectoral fin

Pelvic fin

Anal fin

Tail fin

129 Hammerhead sharks have a hammer-shaped head! With

a nostril and an eye on each end of the "hammer," they swing their head from side to side. This gives them double the chance to see and sniff out any signs of a tasty catch.

▲ Hammerheads prey on other sharks and rays, bony fish, crabs and lobsters, octopus, and squid.

Whales and dolphins

130 **The biggest animal on the planet lives in the oceans.** It is the blue whale, measuring about 90 feet in length and weighing up to 210 tons. It feeds by filtering tiny, shrimplike creatures called krill from the water—about four tons of krill a day! Like other great whales, it has special, sievelike parts in its mouth called baleen plates.

▶ The blue whale can be found in every ocean except the Arctic.

131 Killer whales play with their food. They especially like to catch baby seals, which they toss into the air before eating. Killer whales are not true whales, but are the largest dolphins. They have teeth for chewing, instead of baleen plates.

▼ As the sperm whale surfaces, it pushes out stale air through its blowhole. It fills its lungs with fresh air and dives down again.

132 Whales and dolphins have to come to the surface for air. This is because they are mammals, like we are. Sperm whales hold their breath the longest. They have been known to stay underwater for nearly two hours.

133 Dolphins and whales sing songs to communicate. The noisiest is the humpback whale, whose wailing noises can be heard for hundreds of miles. The sweetest is the beluga—nicknamed the "sea canary." Songs are used to attract a mate, or just to keep track of each other.

▲ The beluga is a type of white whale. It makes a range of noises—whistles, clangs, chirps, and moos!

135 Moby-Dick was a famous white whale. It featured in *Moby-Dick* (1851), a book by Herman Melville about a white sperm whale and a whaler called Captain Ahab.

134 The narwhal has a horn like a unicorn's. This Arctic whale has a long, twirly tooth that spirals out of its head. The males use this tusk as a weapon when they are fighting over females.

▲ A male narwhal's tusk can grow to over 7 feet long.

I DON'T BELIEVE IT!

Barnacles are shellfish. They attach themselves to ships' hulls, or the bodies of gray whales and other large sea animals.

Sleek swimmers

136 Whales and dolphins are not the only sea mammals. Seals, sea lions, and walruses are warm-blooded mammals that have adapted to ocean life. These creatures are known as pinnipeds, meaning they have flippers instead of legs. They also have streamlined bodies and a layer of fatty blubber under the skin, to keep them warm in chilly waters.

▼ Most seals live in cold waters. These crabeater seals live in Antarctica, as do leopard, Weddell, and fur seals. Northern seals, which live around the Arctic, include harp and bearded seals.

▼ Fights between male elephant seals during the breeding season can be extremely violent.

137 Elephant seals are well-named—they are truly enormous! Southern elephant seal males can weigh over 3.8 tons, while their northern cousins weigh at least 2.2 tons. During their three-month-long breeding season, males stay ashore to fight off rivals. Unable to hunt for fish, some lose as much as half their body weight.

▼ Walruses use their tusks as weapons. They are also used to make breathing holes in the ice, and to help the walrus pull itself out of the water.

138 **Walruses seem to change color!** When a walrus is in the water, it appears pale brown or even white. This is because blood drains from the skin's surface to stop the body losing heat. On land, the blood returns to the skin and walruses can look reddish brown or pink.

I DON'T BELIEVE IT!

Leopard seals sing in their sleep! These seals, found in the Antarctic, chirp and whistle while they snooze.

▼ Anchored to the kelp, a sea otter is free to rest.

139 **Sea otters anchor themselves when they sleep.** These playful creatures live off the Pacific coast among huge forests of giant seaweed called kelp. When they sleep, they wrap a strand of kelp around their body to stop them being washed out to sea.

Ocean reptiles

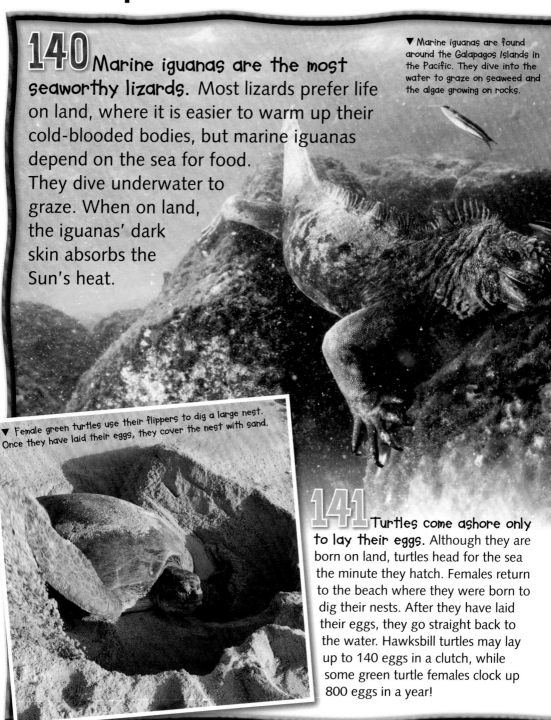

140 **Marine iguanas are the most seaworthy lizards.** Most lizards prefer life on land, where it is easier to warm up their cold-blooded bodies, but marine iguanas depend on the sea for food. They dive underwater to graze. When on land, the iguanas' dark skin absorbs the Sun's heat.

▼ Marine iguanas are found around the Galapagos Islands in the Pacific. They dive into the water to graze on seaweed and the algae growing on rocks.

▼ Female green turtles use their flippers to dig a large nest. Once they have laid their eggs, they cover the nest with sand.

141 **Turtles come ashore only to lay their eggs.** Although they are born on land, turtles head for the sea the minute they hatch. Females return to the beach where they were born to dig their nests. After they have laid their eggs, they go straight back to the water. Hawksbill turtles may lay up to 140 eggs in a clutch, while some green turtle females clock up 800 eggs in a year!

QUIZ
1. Where are marine iguanas found?
2. Why do turtles come ashore?
3. Where do banded sea snakes search for food?
4. How deep can leatherback turtles dive?

Answers:
1. Around the Galapagos Islands 2. To lay their eggs 3. Coral reefs 4. Up to 3,900 feet

142
There are venomous (poisonous) snakes in the sea. Most stay close to land and come ashore to lay their eggs. Banded sea snakes, for example, cruise around coral reefs in search of their favorite food—eels. But the yellow-bellied sea snake never leaves the water. It gives birth to live babies in the open ocean.

▶ Banded sea snakes use venom (poison) to stun their prey.

▼ The yellow-bellied sea snake uses its colorful underside to attract fish. It then darts back —so the fish are next to its open mouth!

Banded sea snake

Yellow-bellied sea snake

▼ Leatherbacks are the biggest turtles in the world and can grow to 7 feet in length.

143
Leatherback turtles dive up to 3,900 feet for food. They hold the record for being the biggest sea turtles and for making the deepest dives. Leatherbacks feed mostly on jellyfish, but their diet also includes mollusks, crabs, lobsters, and starfish.

Icy depths

144 Few creatures can survive in the dark, icy-cold ocean depths. Food is so hard to come by, the deep-sea anglerfish does not waste energy chasing prey. It has a stringy "fishing rod" with a glowing tip that extends from its dorsal fin or hangs above its jaw. This attracts smaller fish to the anglerfish's big mouth.

▲ Anglerfish are black or brown for camouflage. Only their glowing "fishing rod" is visible in the gloom.

Lantern fish

Cookie-cutter shark

Hatchet fish

145 Some deep-sea fish glow in the dark. As well as tempting prey, light also confuses predators. About 1,500 different deep-sea fish give off light. The lantern fish's whole body glows. The hatchet fish produces light along its belly and has silvery scales on its sides, which reflect light, confusing predators. Just the belly of the cookie-cutter shark gives off a ghostly glow.

◀ The light created by deep-sea fish, or by bacteria living on their bodies, is known as biological light, or bioluminescence.

146
Black swallowers are greedy-guts! These strange fish are just 10 inches long but can eat fish far bigger than themselves. Their loose jaws unhinge to fit over the prey. Then the stretchy body expands to take in their enormous meal.

147
Viperfish have teeth that are invisible in the dark. They swim around with their jaws wide open. Deep-sea shrimp often see nothing until they are right inside the viperfish's mouth.

▶ The viperfish is named for its long, snakelike fangs.

148
On the seabed, there are worms as long as cars! These are giant tubeworms and they cluster around hot spots on the ocean floor. They feed on tiny particles that they filter from the water.

▲ The black swallower's stomach can stretch to take in prey twice its length.

▼ Bacteria inside the tubeworm turn minerals into food that the worm needs to survive.

Plume

Bacteria

Heart

Blood Vessel

Tube

I DON'T BELIEVE IT!
Female deep-sea anglerfish grow to 47 inches in length, but the males are a tiny 2.3 inches!

Amazing journeys

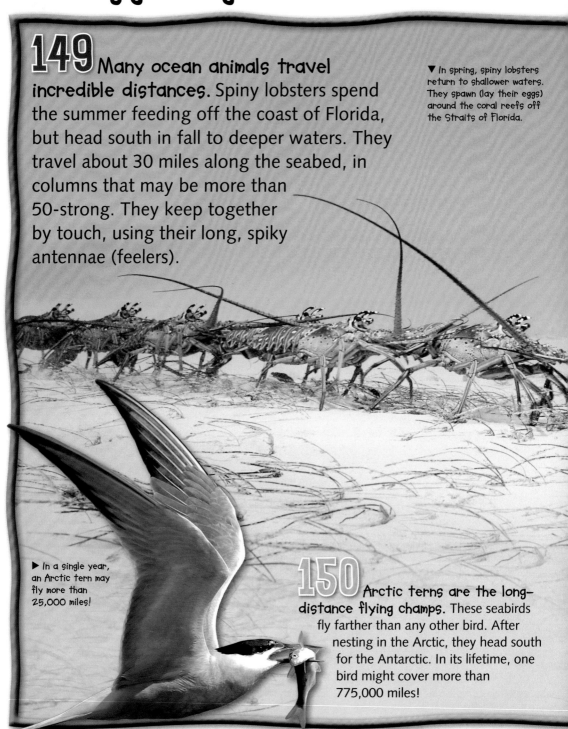

149 **Many ocean animals travel incredible distances.** Spiny lobsters spend the summer feeding off the coast of Florida, but head south in fall to deeper waters. They travel about 30 miles along the seabed, in columns that may be more than 50-strong. They keep together by touch, using their long, spiky antennae (feelers).

▼ In spring, spiny lobsters return to shallower waters. They spawn (lay their eggs) around the coral reefs off the Straits of Florida.

▶ In a single year, an Arctic tern may fly more than 25,000 miles!

150 **Arctic terns are the long-distance flying champs.** These seabirds fly farther than any other bird. After nesting in the Arctic, they head south for the Antarctic. In its lifetime, one bird might cover more than 775,000 miles!

① Gray whales travel south to Mexico in winter to have their babies.

② In summer the whales swim back to the food-rich waters off the coast of Alaska.

▲ Gray whales spend summer in the Bering Sea, feeding on tiny, shrimplike creatures called amphipods. They spend their breeding season, December to March, in warmer waters.

151 Gray whales migrate, or travel, farther than any other mammal. There are two main gray whale populations in the Pacific. One spends summer off the Alaskan coast. In winter, they migrate south to Mexico to breed. The whales may swim nearly 12,500 miles in a year. The other gray whale group spends summer off the coast of Russia, then travels south to Korea.

I DON'T BELIEVE IT!
Eels and salmon swim thousands of miles from the sea to spawn in the same river nurseries where they were born.

▲ As soon as they are born, loggerhead hatchlings crawl down to the water, to avoid being picked off by hungry gulls or crabs.

152 Baby loggerhead turtles make a two-year journey. They are born on beaches in Japan. The hatchlings hurry down to the sea and set off across the Pacific to Mexico, a journey of 6,200 miles. They spend about five years there before returning to Japan to breed.

On the wing

Quiz

1. How long is the wingspan of an albatross?
2. Where do puffins dig their burrows?
3. How do gannets dive for fish?
4. What color is a male frigate bird's pouch?

Answers:
1. Around 10 feet 2. On clifftops
3. Headfirst into the ocean 4. Bright red

153 Wandering albatrosses are the biggest seabirds. An albatross has a wingspan of around 10 feet—about the length of a family car! These seabirds are so large, they take off by launching from a cliff. Albatrosses spend months at sea. To feed, they land on the sea, where they sit and catch creatures such as squid.

▶ Albatrosses are such expert gliders that they can even sleep on the wing.

▼ Puffins often scrape their own burrows on clifftops, or they may take over an abandoned rabbit hole.

154 Puffins nest in burrows. While many birds jostle for space on a high cliff edge, puffins dig a burrow on the clifftop. Here, they lay a single egg. Both parents feed the chick for the first 6 weeks.

155 Gannets wear air-bag shock absorbers. The gannet's feeding technique is to plummet headfirst into the ocean and catch a fish in its beak. It dives at high-speed and hits the water hard. Luckily, the gannet's head is protected with sacs of air that absorb most of the shock.

156 Frigate birds puff up a balloon for their mate. Male frigate birds have a bright-red pouch on their throat. They inflate, or blow up, the pouch as part of their display to attract a female.

▲ When a gannet spots its meal, it dives into the water at high speed to catch it.

▼ A frigate bird shows off to its mate.

▶ A blue-footed booby displays its blue feet.

157 Boobies dance to attract a mate. There are two types of booby, blue- or red-footed. The dancing draws attention to the male's colorful feet. Perhaps this stops the females from mating with the wrong type of bird.

Perfect penguins

158 Macaroni, Gentoo, Chinstrap, and Emperor are all types of penguin. There are 17 different types in total, and most live around the Antarctic. Penguins feed on fish, squid, and krill. Their black-and-white plumage is important camouflage. Seen from above, a penguin's black back blends in with the water. The white belly is hard to distinguish from the sunlit surface of the sea.

▼ King penguins live near Antarctica. Like all penguins, they have a layer of fat under their feathers to protect them in the icy water.

159 Penguins can swim, but not fly. They have oily, waterproof feathers and flipperlike wings. Instead of lightweight, hollow bones—like a flying bird's—some penguins have solid, heavy bones. This enables them to stay underwater longer when diving for food. Emperor penguins can stay under for 15 minutes or more.

160 Some penguins build stone circles. This is the way that Adélie and Gentoo penguins build nests on the shingled shores where they breed. First, they scrape out a small dip with their flippered feet and then they surround the hollow with a circle of pebbles.

▲ An Adélie penguin builds its nest from stones and small rocks.

▼ The different types of penguin vary in shape, size and appearance.

Rockhopper   Macaroni   Royal   Chinstrap   Gentoo

161 **Emperor penguin dads balance an egg on their feet.** They do this to keep their egg off the Antarctic ice, where it would freeze. The female leaves her mate with the egg for the whole two months that it takes to hatch. The male has to go without food during this time. When the chick hatches, the mother returns and both parents help to raise it.

▶ A downy Emperor penguin chick cannot find its own food in the sea until it has grown its waterproof, adult plumage. In the meantime, its parents feed and care for it.

Harvests from the sea

162 Oysters come from beds —and lobsters from pots! The animals in the oceans feed other sea creatures, and they feed us, too! To gather oysters, fishermen raise them on trays or poles in the water. First, they collect oyster larvae, or babies. They attract them by putting out sticks hung with shells. Lobster larvae are too difficult to collect, but the adults are caught in pots filled with fish bait.

▲ Bait is placed in lobster pots like these. Once a lobster has entered, it can't escape.

163 Some farmers grow seaweed. Seaweed is delicious to eat, and is also a useful ingredient in products such as ice cream and plant fertilizer. In shallow, tropical waters, people grow their own on plots of seabed.

▼ A woman harvests seaweed on a farm on the coast of Zanzibar, East Africa.

164 Sea minerals are big business.

Minerals are useful substances that we mine from the ground—and oceans are full of them! The most valuable are oil and gas, which are pumped from the seabed and piped ashore or transported in huge supertankers. Salt is another important mineral. In hot, low-lying areas, people build walls to hold shallow pools of sea water. The water dries up in the sun, leaving behind crystals of salt.

165 There are gemstones under the sea.

Pearls are made by oysters. If a grain of sand is lodged inside an oyster's shell, it irritates its soft body. The oyster coats the sand with a substance called nacre, which is also used to line the inside of the shell. Over the years, more nacre builds up and the pearl gets bigger.

▲ The oil platform's welded-steel legs rest on the seabed. They support the platform around 50 feet above the surface of the water.

▶ An oyster's shell must be pried open with a knife to get to the pearl inside.

WEATHER

166 Rain, sunshine, snow, and storms are all types of weather. Different weather is caused by what is happening in the atmosphere— the air around and above us. In some parts of the world, the weather changes every day, but in others it is mostly the same.

▼ The colors on this map indicate the different types of climate found around the world.

EUROPE

NORTH AMERICA

AFRICA

Equator

SOUTH AMERICA

Cold temperate
Cold winter with snow, cool dry summer

Wet temperate
Cool winter, warm summer, rain all year round

Mountainous
Gets steadily colder as land gets higher

Temperate grassland
Cold winter with snow, hot, dry summer

Tropical forest
Hot and rainy all
year round

Polar
Sub-zero temperatures
and snow all year round

Desert
Hot in day, cold at night,
very little rain

ASIA

Dry temperate
Mild winter with rain,
hot dry summer

OCEANIA

NTARCTICA

Tropical
Hot all year round
with seasonal rain

▲ In general, the warmest climates are found near the Equator.
The closer to the Poles—the two points at opposite ends of
the Earth—the cooler the climate. Weather and climate affect
how animals, plants, and people survive and behave.

167 Tropical, temperate, and
polar are all types of climate. Climate
is the name we give to patterns of weather
over a period of time. Near the Equator (an
imaginary belt around the middle of the
Earth), the weather is mostly hot
and steamy. We call this a
tropical climate. Near the
North and South Poles, ice
lies on the ground all year
round and there are biting-cold
blizzards. This is a polar climate. Most of
the world has a temperate climate—a mix
of cold and warm seasons.

Four seasons

168 **The reason we have seasons lies in space.** The pull of the Sun's gravity means Earth orbits (travels around) the Sun. One orbit takes one year to complete. Over the year, Earth's tilt causes first one and then the other Pole to lean toward the Sun, and this gives us seasons. For example, in June the North Pole is tilted toward the Sun. The Sun heats the northern half of the Earth and it is summer.

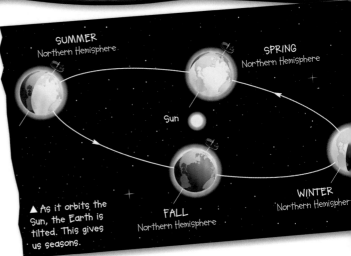

SUMMER
Northern Hemisphere

SPRING
Northern Hemisphere

Sun

WINTER
Northern Hemispher

FALL
Northern Hemisphere

▲ As it orbits the Sun, the Earth is tilted. This gives us seasons.

169 **When it is summer in Argentina, it is winter in Canada.** In December, the South Pole leans toward the Sun. Places in the southern half of the world, such as Argentina, have summer. At the same time, places in the northern half, such as Canada, have winter.

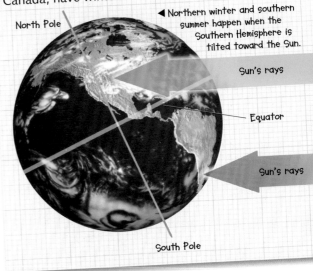

◄ Northern winter and southern summer happen when the Southern Hemisphere is tilted toward the Sun.

North Pole

Sun's rays

Equator

Sun's rays

South Pole

I DON'T BELIEVE IT!

When the Sun shines all day in the far north, there is 24-hour night in the far south.

▼ Near the North Pole, the Sun never sets below the horizon on Midsummer's Day.

170 Daylight can last for 24 hours!
Night and day happen because Earth is spinning as it circles the Sun. At the height of summer, places near the North Pole are so tilted toward the Sun that it is light all day long. In northern Sweden, on Midsummer's Day, it is light for 24 hours because the Sun never quite disappears below the horizon.

▶ Trees that lose their leaves in fall are called deciduous. Evergreens are trees that keep their leaves all year round.

FALL

Leaves change color and start to fall. Fruits ripen.

WINTER

Branches are bare.

SUMMER

Flowering trees are in full bloom. Some have a second growth spurt.

SPRING

Leaf buds start to grow. The leaves soon open and flowers bloom.

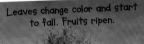

171 Some forests change color in the fall.
Fall comes between summer and winter. Trees prepare for the cold winter months ahead by losing their leaves. First, though, they suck back the precious green chlorophyll, or dye, in their leaves, making them turn glorious shades of red, orange, and brown.

Fewer seasons

172 Monsoons are winds that carry heavy rains. During the hot, rainy tropical summer, the Sun warms the sea, causing huge banks of cloud to form. These are blown by monsoon winds toward land. Once they hit the continent, rain can pour for weeks.

▲ When monsoon rains are especially heavy, they can cause chaos. Streets turn to rivers and sometimes people's homes are washed away.

173 Monsoons happen mainly in Asia. However, there are parts of the Americas, close to the Equator, that also have a rainy season. Winds can carry heavy rain clouds, causing flash floods in the southwestern deserts of the US. The floods happen because the land has been baked hard during the dry season, so water doesn't drain away.

POTENTIAL FLASH FLOOD AREAS

NEXT 6 MILES

◄ This sign warns of flash flooding in California, US.

174 **Many parts of the tropics have two seasons, not four.** In the parts of the world closest to the Equator it is always hot, as these places are constantly facing the Sun. However, Earth's movement affects the position of a great band of cloud. In June, the tropical areas north of the Equator have the strongest heat and the heaviest rainstorms. In December, it is the turn of the areas south of the Equator.

Tropic of Cancer

Equator

Tropic of Capricorn

▲ The tropics lie either side of the Equator, between lines of latitude called the Tropic of Cancer and the Tropic of Capricorn.

QUIZ

1. What are monsoons?
2. On which continent do most monsoons occur?
3. How many seasons are there in the tropics?
4. How much rainfall do tropical rain forests usually have in a year?

Answers:
1. Winds that carry heavy rains 2. Asia 3. Two 4. About 80 inches

◄ Daily rainfall feeds lush rain forest vegetation and countless waterfalls in the mountains of Costa Rica.

175 **Tropical rain forests have rainy weather all year round.** There is usually about 80 inches of rainfall in a year. Rain forests still have a wet and a dry season, but the wet season is even wetter! Some parts of the rain forest can become flooded during the wet season, as the heavy rain makes rivers overflow their banks.

What a scorcher!

176 All of our heat comes from the Sun. The Sun is a star—a ball of burning gases. The heat rays it gives off travel 93 million miles through space to reach Earth. The rays cool down on the journey, but are still hot enough to scorch Earth.

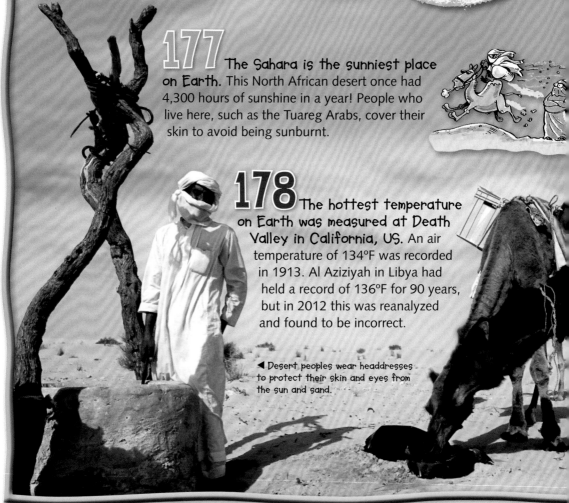

177 The Sahara is the sunniest place on Earth. This North African desert once had 4,300 hours of sunshine in a year! People who live here, such as the Tuareg Arabs, cover their skin to avoid being sunburnt.

178 The hottest temperature on Earth was measured at Death Valley in California, US. An air temperature of 134°F was recorded in 1913. Al Aziziyah in Libya had held a record of 136°F for 90 years, but in 2012 this was reanalyzed and found to be incorrect.

◄ Desert peoples wear headdresses to protect their skin and eyes from the sun and sand.

179
The Sun can trick your eyes. Sometimes, as sunlight passes through our atmosphere, it hits layers of air at different temperatures. When this happens, the air bends the light and can trick our eyes into seeing something that is not there. This is a mirage. For example, what looks like a pool of water might really be part of the sky reflected on to the land.

▲ A mirage is just a trick of the light. It can make us see something that is not really there.

180
Too much sun brings drought. Clear skies and sunshine are not always good news. Without rain, crops wither, and people and their animals go hungry.

181
One terrible drought made a "Dust Bowl." Settlements in the American Midwest were devastated by a long drought during the 1930s. As crops died, there were no roots to hold the soil together. The dry earth turned to dust and some farms simply blew away!

▼ During the 1930s, dust storms caused by drought in Oklahoma, US, covered fields in layers of dust.

Warm water

OCEANIA

PACIFIC OCEAN

SOUTH AMERICA

Cold water

▲ El Niño has been known to cause violent weather conditions. It returns on average every four years.

182
All sorts of things affect our weather and climate. The movements of a sea current called El Niño have been blamed for causing flooding and terrible drought—which can lead to unstoppable forest fires.

Our atmosphere

KEY

1. Exosphere
   118 to 590 miles

2. Thermosphere
   49 to 118 miles

3. Mesosphere
   31 to 49 miles

4. Stratosphere
   6 to 31 miles

5. Troposphere
   0 to 6 miles

183 **Earth is wrapped in a blanket of air called the atmosphere, which is hundreds of miles thick.** The atmosphere keeps heat in at night, and during the day forms a sunscreen, protecting us from the Sun's fierce rays. Without it there would be no weather.

184 **Most weather happens in the troposphere.** This is the layer of atmosphere that stretches from the ground to around 6 miles above your head. The higher in the troposphere you go, the cooler the air. Because of this, clouds are most likely to form here. Clouds with flattened tops show just where the troposphere meets the next layer, the stratosphere.

▶ This view of the Earth from the International Space Station, which orbits the Earth, shows the atmosphere as a thin, wispy layer.

Low-level satellites orbit within the exosphere.

The Northern and Southern Lights—the auroras—are formed in the thermosphere.

Meteors entering the atmosphere burn up in the mesosphere, causing "shooting stars."

Aeroplanes either fly high in the troposphere, or in the lower levels of the stratosphere.

Weather forms in the troposphere.

▲ The atmosphere stretches right into space. Scientists have split it into five layers, or spheres.

185 Molecules (tiny particles) in the air are constantly bumping into each other. The more they do this, the greater the air pressure. There are usually more collisions lower in the troposphere, because gravity pulls the molecules toward Earth's surface. The higher you go, the lower the air pressure, and the less oxygen there is in the air.

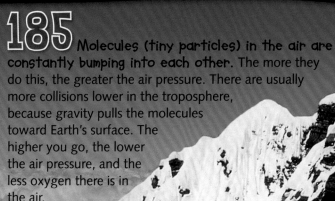

186 Warmth makes air move. When heat from the Sun warms the molecules in air, they move faster and spread out more. This makes the air lighter, so it rises in the sky, creating low pressure. As it gets higher, the air cools. The molecules slow down and become heavier again, so they start to sink back to Earth.

HIGH PRESSURE

LOW PRESSURE

Cool air sinking

Center of high pressure

Air flow moves in clockwise direction

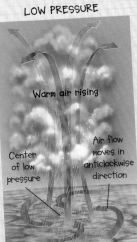

Warm air rising

Center of low pressure

Air flow moves in anticlockwise direction

▲ A high pressure weather system gives us warmer weather, while low pressure gives us cooler, more unsettled weather. (In the Northern Hemisphere, air flows anticlockwise in a low pressure system, and clockwise in high pressure. In the Southern Hemisphere, it is the opposite.)

▲ At high altitudes there is less oxygen. That is why mountaineers often wear breathing equipment.

Clouds and rain

187 **Water goes on a journey called the water cycle.** As the Sun heats the ocean's surface, some seawater turns to vapor and rises. As it rises, it cools and turns back into droplets, which join to make clouds. The droplets continue forming bigger drops and eventually fall as rain. Some is soaked up by land, but a lot finds its way back to the sea.

KEY
1 Water evaporates from the sea
2 Clouds form
3 Water is given off by trees
4 Rain falls, filling rivers
5 Rivers run back to the sea

188 **Some mountains are so tall that their summits are hidden by cloud.** They can even affect the weather. When moving air hits a mountain slope it is forced upward, causing its temperature to drop, and clouds to form.

▼ The peak of Chapaeva, in the Tian Shan mountain range in Asia, can be seen above the clouds.

WARM AIR

▼ Water moves in a continuous cycle between the ocean, atmosphere, and land.

189 Clouds release energy. When water vapor

becomes water droplets and forms clouds, a small amount of heat energy is given out into the atmosphere. Then, when the droplets fall as rain, kinetic (movement) energy is released as the rain hits the ground.

RAIN GAUGE

You will need:
jam jar   waterproof marker pen
ruler   notebook   pen

Put the jar outside. At the same time each day, mark the rainwater level on the jar with your pen. At the end of a week, empty the jar. Measure and record how much rain fell each day and over the whole week.

▶ Virga happens when rain reaches a layer of dry air. The rain droplets turn back into water vapor in mid-air, and seem to disappear.

190 Some rain

never reaches the ground. The raindrops turn back into water vapor because they hit a layer of super-dry air. You can actually see the drops falling like a curtain from the cloud, but the curtain stops in mid-air. This type of weather is called virga.

Not just fluffy

191 **Clouds come in all shapes and sizes.** Scientists divide them into three basic types according to their shape and height above the ground. Wispy cirrus clouds form high in the troposphere and rarely mean rain. Flat, layered stratus clouds may produce drizzle or a sprinkling of snow. Soft, fluffy cumulus clouds usually bring rain.

192 **Cumulus humilis clouds are the smallest heap-shaped clouds.** They are too small to produce rain but they can grow into much bigger, rain-carrying cumulus clouds. The biggest cumulus clouds, called cumulonimbus, bring heavy rainfall.

Cirrus
Thin, wispy high-level clouds, sometimes called "mare's tails"

Cumulonimbus
Towering gray-white clouds that produce heavy rainfall

Cumulus
Billowing clouds with flat bases

Nimbostratus
Dense layer of low, gray rain clouds

▶ The main classes of cloud—cirrus, cumulus, and stratus— were named in the 1800s. An amateur British weather scientist called Luke Howard identified the different types.

Cirrocumulus
Ripples or rows of small
white clouds at high altitude

Contrails
The white streaks
created by planes

Altocumulus
Small globular clouds
at middle altitude

193 Not all clouds are made by nature. Contrails are streaky clouds that a plane leaves behind it as it flies. They are made of water vapor that comes from the plane's engines. The second it hits the cold air, the vapor turns into ice crystals, leaving a trail of white cloud.

Altostratus
Layered gray middle-level
cloud with no visible holes

194 Sometimes the sky is filled with white patches of cloud that look like shimmering fish scales. These are called mackerel skies. It takes lots of gusty wind to break the cloud into these little patches, and so mackerel skies are usually a sign of changeable weather.

Stratocumulus
Gray clouds in patches or
globules that may join together

◀ A mackerel sky over Calanais stone circle in Scotland.

Stratus
Continuous low cloud near,
but not touching, the ground

Flood warning

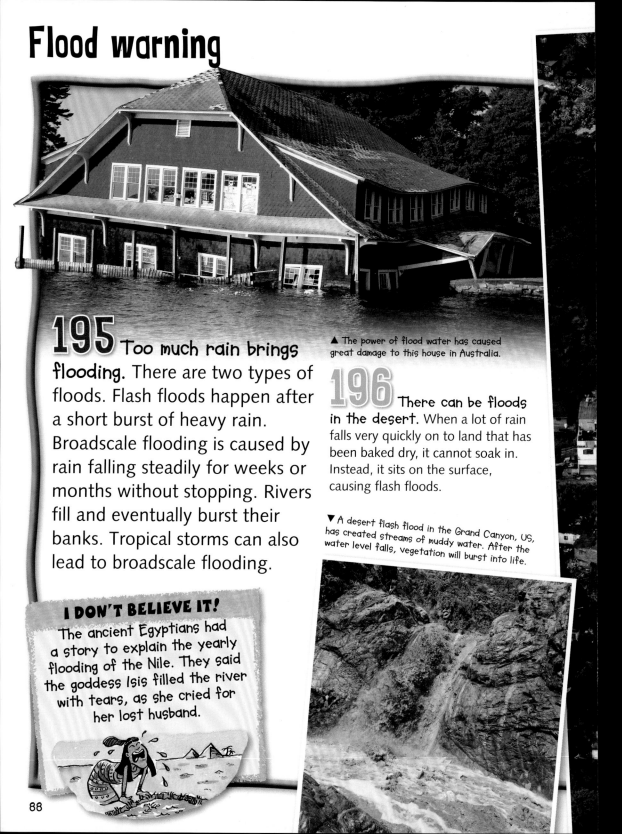

195 **Too much rain brings flooding.** There are two types of floods. Flash floods happen after a short burst of heavy rain. Broadscale flooding is caused by rain falling steadily for weeks or months without stopping. Rivers fill and eventually burst their banks. Tropical storms can also lead to broadscale flooding.

▲ The power of flood water has caused great damage to this house in Australia.

196 **There can be floods in the desert.** When a lot of rain falls very quickly on to land that has been baked dry, it cannot soak in. Instead, it sits on the surface, causing flash floods.

▼ A desert flash flood in the Grand Canyon, US, has created streams of muddy water. After the water level falls, vegetation will burst into life.

I DON'T BELIEVE IT!

The ancient Egyptians had a story to explain the yearly flooding of the Nile. They said the goddess Isis filled the river with tears, as she cried for her lost husband.

197 The Bible tells of a terrible flood, and how a man named Noah was saved. Explorers recently found evidence of the flood—a sunken beach 460 feet below the surface of the Black Sea. There are ruins of houses, dating back to 5600 BC. Stories of a flood in ancient times do not only appear in the Bible—the Babylonians and Greeks told of one, too.

▼ In the Bible, Noah survived the Great Flood by building a huge wooden boat called an ark.

198 When rain mixes with earth it makes mud. On a mountainside, with no tree roots to hold soil together, rain can cause an avalanche of mud. In 1985 flooding in Colombia, South America, caused a terrible mudslide that buried 23,000 people from the town of Armero.

◄ Torrential rain in Brazil caused this mudslide, which swept away part of a village.

Deep freeze

▶ This truck has become stuck in a snow drift. Falling snow is made worse by strong winds, which can form deep drifts.

199 Snow is made of tiny ice crystals. At very cold air temperatures—around 32°F—water droplets in clouds freeze into tiny ice crystals. If these clump together they fall as snowflakes.

▼ A snowflake that is a couple of inches across will be made up of lots of crystals, like these.

200 No two snowflakes are the same. This is because snowflakes are made up of ice crystals, and every ice crystal is as unique as your fingerprint. Most crystals look like six-pointed stars, but they come in other shapes too.

201 Black ice is not really black. Drizzle or rain turns to ice when it touches freezing-cold ground. This "black" ice is see-through, and hard to spot against a road's dark tarmac. It is also very slippery, creating dangerous driving conditions.

I DON'T BELIEVE IT
Antarctica is the coldest place on Earth. Temperatures of −128°F have been recorded there.

202

Avalanches are like giant snowballs. They can happen after lots of snow falls on a mountain. The slightest movement or sudden noise can jolt the pile of snow into moving down the slope. As it crashes down, the avalanche picks up extra snow and can end up large enough to bury whole towns.

▲ An avalanche gathers speed as it thunders down the mountainside.

203

Marksmen shoot at snowy mountains. One way to prevent deadly avalanches is to stop too much snow from building up. In mountainous areas, marksmen set off mini avalanches on purpose. They make sure people are out of the danger zone, then fire guns to trigger a snowslide.

▼ Antarctica is a frozen wilderness. The ice piles up to form amazing shapes.

204

Ice can stay frozen for millions of years. At the North and South Poles, the weather never warms up enough for all of the ice to thaw. When fresh snow falls, it presses down on the snow already there, forming thick sheets. Some ice may not have melted for a million years or more.

When the wind blows

205 Wind is moving air. Air is constantly moving from areas of high pressure to areas of low pressure. The bigger the difference in pressure between the two areas, the faster the wind blows.

▶ In open, exposed areas, trees can be forced into strange shapes by the wind.

206 World wind patterns are called global winds. The most famous are the trade winds that blow toward the Equator. Well-known local winds include the cold, dry mistral that blows down to southern France, and the hot, dry sirroco that blows north of the Sahara.

▼ This map shows the pattern of the world's main winds.

North Pole

Polar easterlies

Westerlies

Equator

Trade winds

Westerlies

Polar easterlies

South Pole

207 Trade winds blow from east to west, above and below the Equator. In the tropics, air is moving to an area of low pressure at the Equator. The winds blow toward the Equator, from the southeast in the Southern Hemisphere, and the northeast in the Northern Hemisphere. Their name comes from their importance to traders, when goods traveled across the oceans by sailing ship.

208 **You can tell how windy it is by looking at the leaves on a tree.** Wind strength is measured on the Beaufort Scale, named after the Irish admiral who devised it. The scale is based on the visible effects of wind, and ranges from Force 0, meaning total calm, to Force 12, which is a hurricane.

209 **Wind can bring very changeable weather.** The Föhn wind, which sometimes blows across Switzerland, Austria, and Bavaria in southern Germany, brings with it significant and rapid rises in temperature, sometimes by as much as 85°F in a matter of hours. This has been blamed for various illnesses, including bouts of madness!

210 **Wind can turn on your TV.** People can harness the energy of wind to make electricity for our homes. Tall turbines are positioned in windy places. As the wind turns the turbine, the movement powers a generator and produces electrical energy.

▼ Wind energy doesn't create any harmful pollution, and it will never run out.

The Beaufort Scale

Force 0: Calm
Smoke rises straight up

Force 1: Light air
Wind motion visible in smoke

Force 2: Light breeze
Leaves rustle

Force 3: Gentle breeze
Twigs move, light flags flap

Force 4: Moderate breeze
Small branches move

Force 5: Fresh breeze
Bushes and small trees sway

Force 6: Strong breeze
Large branches in motion

Force 7: Near gale
Whole trees sway

Force 8: Gale
Difficult to walk or move, twigs break

Force 9: Strong gale
Tiles and chimneys may be blown from rooftops

Force 10: Storm
Trees uprooted

Force 11: Violent storm
Widespread damage to buildings

Force 12: Hurricane
Severe devastation

Thunderbolts and lightning

211 **Thunderstorms are most likely to occur in summer.** Warm, moist air rises and forms cumulonimbus clouds. Inside the clouds, water droplets and ice crystals move about, building up positive and negative electrical charges. Electricity flows between the charges, creating a flash (lightning). The air heated by the lightning expands, causing a loud noise, or thunderclap.

▼ Cloud-to-cloud lightning is called sheet lightning. Lightning traveling from the cloud to the ground, as shown here, is called fork lightning.

HOW CLOSE?

Lightning and thunder happen at the same time, but light travels faster than sound. Count the seconds between the lightning flash and thunderclap and divide by five. This is how many miles away the storm is.

▼ Dramatic lightning flashes in Arizona, US, light up the sky.

212 **Lightning comes in different colors.** If there is rain in the thundercloud, the lightning looks red or pink, and if there's hail, it looks blue. Lightning can also be yellow or white.

▼ Hailstones can be huge! These ones are as big as a golf ball.

213 Chunks of ice called hailstones can fall from thunderclouds. The biggest hailstones fell in Gopaljang, Bangladesh, in 1986 and weighed 2.25 pounds each!

214 A person can survive a lightning strike. Lightning is very dangerous and can give a big enough electric shock to kill you. However, an American park ranger called Roy Sullivan survived being struck seven times.

215 Tall buildings are protected from lightning. Church steeples and other tall structures are often struck by bolts of lightning. This could damage the building, or give electric shocks to people inside, so lightning conductors are placed on the roof. These channel the lightning safely away.

◀ If lightning hits a conductor it is carried safely to the ground.

Eye of the hurricane

216 Wind speeds may reach more than 75 miles an hour. Violent tropical storms occur when strong winds blow into an area of low pressure and start to spin. They develop over warm seas, getting faster until they hit land, and there is no more moist sea air to feed them.

217 The center of a hurricane is calm and still. This part is called the "eye." As the eye of the storm passes over, there is a pause in the terrifying rain and wind.

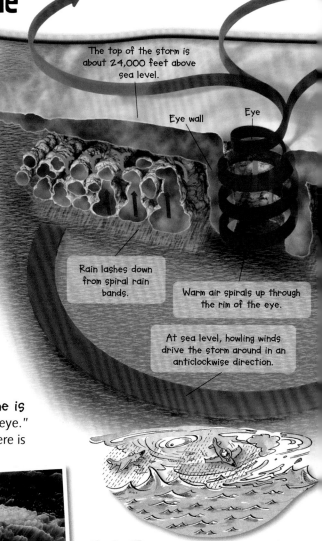

The top of the storm is about 24,000 feet above sea level.

Eye wall

Eye

Rain lashes down from spiral rain bands.

Warm air spirals up through the rim of the eye.

At sea level, howling winds drive the storm around in an anticlockwise direction.

▲ This satellite photograph shows how the storm whirls around the central, still "eye" of the hurricane.

218 Hurricane Hunters fly close to the eye of a hurricane. These are special weather planes that fly into the storm in order to take measurements such as atmospheric pressure. It is a dangerous job for the pilots, but the information they gather helps to predict the hurricane's path—and saves lives.

Top-level winds spread out air over the top of the storm in a clockwise direction.

◀ The huge disk of thunderclouds that makes up a hurricane is hundreds of miles in diameter. The storm spins anticlockwise in the Northern Hemisphere, and clockwise in the Southern Hemisphere.

219 Hurricanes make the sea rise.

As the storm races over the ocean, its strong winds push on the seawater in front of it. This causes seawater to pile up, sometimes more than 30 feet high, which hits the shore as a storm surge. In 1961, the storm surge following Hurricane Hattie washed away Belize City in South America.

▼ Massive waves crash onto shore in Rhode Island, US, during Superstorm Sandy in October 2012. Sandy began as a hurricane, but was downgraded to a storm.

220 Hurricanes have names.

The National Weather Service in the US officially began a naming system in 1954. One of the worst hurricanes was Hurricane Katrina, which battered the US coast from Florida to Texas in August 2005.

221 Typhoons saved the Japanese from Genghis Khan.

The 13th-century Mongol leader made two attempts to invade Japan—and both times, a terrible typhoon battered his fleet of ships and saved the Japanese!

◀ A typhoon prevented Genghis Khan's navy from invading Japan.

Twisting tornadoes

222 Tornadoes are among the most destructive storms. Also known as twisters, these whirling columns of wind form in strong thunderstorms. When the back part of the thundercloud starts spinning, the spinning air forms a funnel that reaches down toward the ground. As it touches the ground, it becomes a tornado.

223 A spinning tornado whizzes along the ground, sucking up everything in its path. It may rip the roofs off houses, and even toss whole buildings into the air. In the 1930s, a twister in Minnesota, US, threw a train carriage full of people over 26 feet into the air!

▶ A tornado can cause great damage to anything in its path, reaching speeds of up to 300 miles an hour.

▶ The shaded area shows Tornado Alley, where there are hundreds of tornadoes each year.

US
Minneapolis
Sioux Falls
Chicago
Denver
Kansas City
Wichita
St Louis
Amarillo
Oklahoma City
Dallas
Houston
New Orleans
MEXICO

224 Tornado Alley is a twister hotspot in the American Midwest.
This is where hot air traveling north from the Gulf of Mexico meets cold polar winds traveling south, and creates huge thunderclouds. Of course, tornadoes can happen anywhere in the world when the conditions are right.

225 A pillar of whirling water can rise out of a lake or the sea.
Waterspouts are spiraling columns of water that can be sucked up by a tornado as it forms over a lake or the sea. They tend to spin more slowly than tornadoes because water is much heavier than air.

◀ Waterspouts can suck up fish from a lake!

226 Dust devils are similar to tornadoes, and form in deserts and other dry dusty areas.
They shift tons of sand and can cause terrible damage—stripping the paintwork from a car in seconds.

◀ A desert dust devil in Amboseli National Park, Kenya.

99

Sky lights

227
Rainbows are caused by sunlight passing through raindrops. The water acts like a glass prism, splitting the light. White light is made up of seven colors—red, orange, yellow, green, blue, indigo, and violet. These colors, from top to bottom, make up the rainbow.

◄ Rainbows are often seen after rain has stopped.

228
Halos can form around the Sun or Moon! If you look at the Sun or Moon through clouds containing tiny ice crystals, they seem to be surrounded by a glowing ring of light.

229
Two rainbows can appear at once. This is caused by the light being reflected twice inside a raindrop. The top rainbow is a reflection of the bottom one, so its colors appear the opposite way round, with the violet band at the top and red at the bottom.

230
Some rainbows appear at night. They happen when falling raindrops split moonlight, rather than sunlight. This sort of rainbow is called a moonbow. They are very rare, and can only be seen in a few places in the world.

◄ A halo around the Sun or Moon can be a sign that a storm is coming.

REMEMBER IT!

Each letter, in order, in the name below gives the first letter of each color of the rainbow—as it appears in the sky:

Roy G. Biv

Red Orange Yellow Green Blue Indigo Violet

▼ Mock suns are also known as parhelia or sundogs.

231
Three suns can appear in the sky. "Mock suns" are two bright spots that appear on either side of the Sun. They often happen at the same time as a halo, and have the same cause—light passing through ice crystals in the air.

▼ An aurora—the most dazzling natural light show on Earth!

232
Auroras are curtains of lights in the sky. They happen in the far north and south of the world when particles from the Sun smash into molecules in the air —at speeds of 990 miles per hour. The lights may be blue, red, yellow, or green.

▼ Although a fogbow is colorless, its inner edge may appear slightly blue and its outer edge slightly red.

233
Some rainbows are just white. Fogbows happen when sunlight passes through a patch of fog. The water droplets in the fog are too small to work like prisms, so the arching bow is white or colorless.

Animal survival

234 Camels can go for two weeks without a drink. They are adapted to life in a hot, dry climate. Camels do not sweat until their body temperature hits 104°F, which helps them to save water. Their humps are fat stores, which are used for energy when food and water is scarce.

◀ Many desert creatures, such as this gecko, come out at night when it is cooler.

235 Lizards lose salt through their noses. Most animals get rid of excess salt in their urine, but lizards, such as iguanas and geckos, live in dry parts of the world. They need to lose as little water from their bodies as possible.

▲ Being able to withstand long periods without water means that camels can survive in the harsh desert environment.

236 Even toads can survive in the desert. The spadefoot toad copes with desert conditions by staying underground in a burrow for most of the year. It only comes to the surface after a shower of rain.

◄ Beneath its gleaming-white fur, the polar bear's skin is black to absorb heat from the Sun.

237 **Polar bears have black skin.** These bears have all sorts of special ways to survive the polar climate. Plenty of body fat and thick fur keeps them snug and warm, while their black skin soaks up as much warmth from the Sun as possible.

238 **Acorn woodpeckers store nuts for winter.** Animals in temperate climates have to be prepared if they are to survive the cold winter months. Acorn woodpeckers turn tree trunks into larders. During fall, when acorns are ripe, the birds collect as many as they can, storing them in holes that they bore into a tree.

◄ Storing acorns for food helps this woodpecker survive the cold winter months.

Myths and legends

239 People once believed the Sun was a god. The sun god was often the most important god of all, bringing light and warmth and ripening crops. Ra, the ancient Egyptian sun god, was head of a group of nine gods. The Aztecs believed that their sun god, Huitzilpochtli, had shown them where to build their capital.

240 Hurricanes are named after a god. The Mayan people lived in Central America, the part of the world that is most affected by hurricanes. Their creator god was called Huracan.

▼ Viking myths tell how Thor was killed in a great battle by a giant serpent.

▲ The Egyptian sun god Ra was often shown with the head of a falcon.

241 The Vikings thought a god brought thunder. Thor was the god of war and thunder, worshiped across what is now Scandinavia. The Vikings pictured Thor as a red-bearded giant. He carried a hammer that produced bolts of lightning. Our day, Thursday, is named in Thor's honor.

242 **People once danced for rain.** In hot countries, people developed dances in the hope that they would bring rain. These were performed by the village shaman (a person thought to have a strong connection to spirits), using wooden instruments such as bullroarers. Sometimes water was sprinkled on the ground. Rain dances are still performed in some countries today.

243 **Totem poles honored the Thunderbird.** Certain tribes of Native Americans built tall, painted totem poles, carved in the image of the Thunderbird. They wanted to keep the spirit happy, because they thought it brought rain to feed the plants.

▶ A Native American totem pole depicting the spirit of the Thunderbird.

MAKE A BULLROARER

You will need:
wooden ruler   string

Ask an adult to drill a hole in one end of the ruler. Thread through the string, and knot it, to stop it slipping through the hole. In an open space, whirl the instrument above your head to create a wind noise!

◀ A Mexican rain-dancer in traditional Mayan costume.

Weather folklore

244
"Red sky at night is the sailor's delight." This is one of the most famous pieces of weather lore and means that a glorious sunset is followed by a fine morning. It is based on the fact that if rain clouds are in the east at sunset, meaning the rain has already passed, they light up red. The saying is also known as "shepherd's delight."

▼ A beautiful sunset could help a sailor to predict the next day's weather.

I DON'T BELIEVE IT!
People used to say that cows lie down when rain is coming—but that's not true. They lie down whether rain is on the way or not!

245
Seaweed can tell us if rain is on the way. Long ago, people looked to nature for clues about the weather. One traditional way of forecasting was to hang up strands of seaweed. If the seaweed stayed slimy, the air was damp and rain was likely. If the seaweed shriveled up, the weather would be dry.

246 "Clear moon, frost soon." This old saying does have some truth in it. If there are few clouds in the sky, the view of the Moon will be clear—and there will also be no blanket of cloud to keep in the Earth's heat. That makes a frost more likely— during the colder months, at least.

▶ The Moon is clearly visible when there are few clouds in the night sky. Its light casts a silvery glow over the Earth.

◀ Early Chinese weather-watchers recorded their observations on pieces of tortoiseshell.

247 The earliest weather records are over 3,000 years old. They were found on a piece of tortoiseshell and had been written by Chinese weather-watchers. The inscriptions describe when it rained or snowed and how windy it was.

▶ Groundhogs emerge from their underground homes in spring following their winter hibernation.

248 Groundhogs tell the weather when they wake. In parts of the US, Groundhog Day is a huge celebration. On February 2, people gather to see the groundhog come out of its burrow. If it is sunny and the groundhog has a shadow, it means there are six more weeks of cold to come. There is no evidence that this is true, though.

Instruments and inventors

▼ This is how the Tower of Winds looks today.

249 The Tower of Winds is the first known weather station. It was built by Andronicus of Cyrrhus in Athens, Greece around 75 BC. It had a wind vane on the roof and a water clock inside. Its eight sides were built to face the points of the compass.

250 The first barometer was made by one of Galileo's students. Barometers measure air pressure. The first person to describe and make an instrument for measuring air pressure was an Italian called Evangelista Torricelli (1608–1647). He had studied under the great scientist Galileo. Torricelli made his barometer in 1643.

◄ Torricelli took a bowl of mercury and placed it under the open end of a glass tube, also filled with mercury. It was the pressure of air on the mercury in the bowl that stopped the mercury in the tube from falling.

251 Weather vanes have been used since around 50 BC. They are placed on the highest point of a building, and have four fixed pointers to show north, south, east, and west. A shape on the top swivels freely, so when the wind blows it points in the direction that the wind is blowing from.

QUIZ

1. What was the Tower of Winds?
2. What did its sides face?
3. What do barometers measure?
4. Who made the first thermometer?

Answers:
1. A weather station 2. The points of the compass 3. Air pressure 4. Gabriel Daniel Fahrenheit

252 A weather house really can predict the weather. It is a type of hygrometer —an instrument that detects how much moisture is in the air. If there is lots, the rainy-day character comes out of the door!

◀ Weather houses have two figures. One comes out when the air is damp, and the other when the air is dry.

253 Fahrenheit made the first thermometer in 1714. Thermometers are instruments that measure temperature. Gabriel Daniel Fahrenheit (1686–1736) invented the thermometer using a blob of mercury sealed in an airtight tube. The Fahrenheit scale for measuring heat was named after him. The Centigrade scale was introduced in 1742 by the Swedish scientist Anders Celsius (1701–1744).

◀ Ships, cockerels, and many other shapes are used to indicate wind direction on weather vanes.

▶ Anders Celsius came from a family of scientists and astronomers.

▲ This early thermometer shows both the Fahrenheit and the Celsius temperature scales.

What's the forecast?

254 **Predicting the weather is called forecasting.** Forecasters study the atmosphere and look at weather patterns. They then use computers to work out what the weather will be like over the coming days.

▲ Meteorologists (weather scientists) use modern technology to track and predict the weather as accurately as possible.

 A cold front is shown by a blue triangle.

 A warm front is shown by a red semicircle.

 Black lines with red semicircles and blue triangles show where a cold front meets a warm front.

White lines called isobars connect places of equal air pressure.

 This symbol shows wind strength and direction. The circle shows how much cloud cover there is.

 This symbol shows that the wind is very strong—look at the three lines on the tail.

This shows an area of calm, with some cloud cover.

▲ Meteorologists call their weather maps synoptic charts. The symbols they use make up a common language for weather scientists all around the world.

WEATHER SYMBOLS

Learn how to represent the weather on your own synoptic charts. Here are some of the basic symbols to get you started. You may come across them in newspapers or while watching television. Can you guess what they mean?

255 **Nations need to share weather data.** By 1865, nearly 60 weather stations across Europe were swapping information. These early meteorologists realized that they needed to present their data using symbols that they could all understand. Today, meteorologists still plot their data on maps called synoptic charts. Lines called isobars link areas of the same air pressure. Symbols indicate temperature and wind.

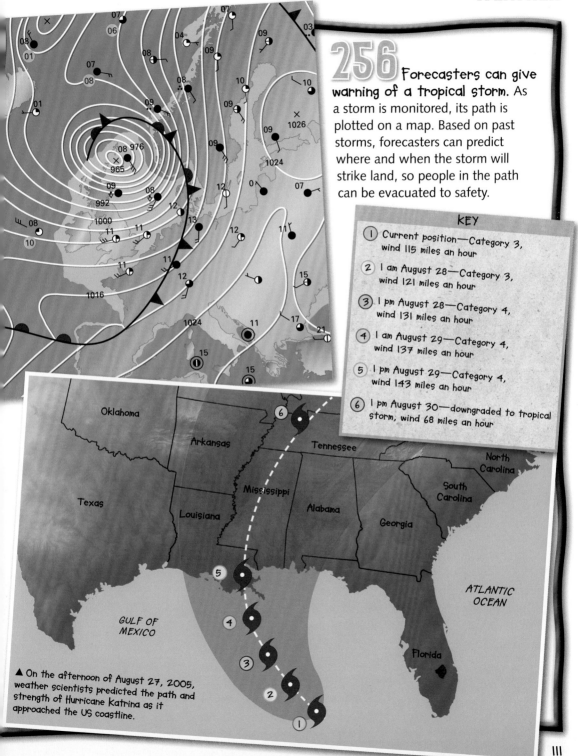

256 Forecasters can give warning of a tropical storm. As a storm is monitored, its path is plotted on a map. Based on past storms, forecasters can predict where and when the storm will strike land, so people in the path can be evacuated to safety.

KEY

1 Current position—Category 3, wind 115 miles an hour

2 1 am August 28—Category 3, wind 121 miles an hour

3 1 pm August 28—Category 4, wind 131 miles an hour

4 1 am August 29—Category 4, wind 137 miles an hour

5 1 pm August 29—Category 4, wind 143 miles an hour

6 1 pm August 30—downgraded to tropical storm, wind 68 miles an hour

▲ On the afternoon of August 27, 2005, weather scientists predicted the path and strength of Hurricane Katrina as it approached the US coastline.

Weather watch

257 Weather balloons carry instruments into the atmosphere. They are filled with helium, which is lighter than air, causing the balloon to rise to a height of almost 18 miles. Instruments attached to the balloon measure the temperature, pressure, and moisture content of the air, and send the information back to meteorologists on the ground. By tracking a balloon's position, they can also measure the speed and direction of high-altitude winds.

▲ NASA's DC-8 plane is a flying laboratory that gathers vital information about different types of weather.

258 Some planes hound the weather. Weather planes provide more detailed information about the atmosphere than balloons can. They can monitor changes in the atmosphere, and detect air pollution. They can also gather information about what causes different types of weather, and help to improve forecasting.

▶ Hundreds of weather balloons around the world are launched every day. This one is being launched into a thunderstorm by a group of weather researchers.

259 Weather satellites provide vital information. From such a long way above the Earth, their cameras can spot the spiraling cloud pattern of a tropical storm while it is still mid-ocean, helping forecasters to issue warnings in good time. Heat-sensitive infrared cameras measure cloud temperature, and are important in forecasting snowfall. Satellite-based radar can also measure the thickness of cloud cover, and the height of ocean waves.

▲ A weather satellite takes photographs of Earth's weather systems from space.

▲ A satellite photo showing two spiral weather systems in the North Atlantic Ocean.

260 Ground-based weather radar that can detect rainfall and wind speed is used at airports. Knowledge of the exact weather conditions is critical for pilots during takeoff and landing. Weather radar is also used to track the formation and path of tornadoes, and at sea, radar can give warning of icebergs.

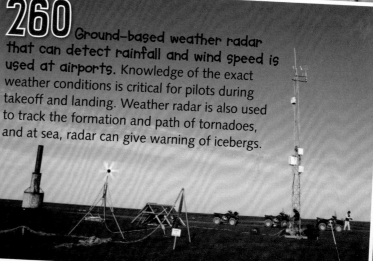

► Weather information is collected from even the remotest parts of the globe. This weather monitoring station is inside the Arctic Circle.

Changing climate

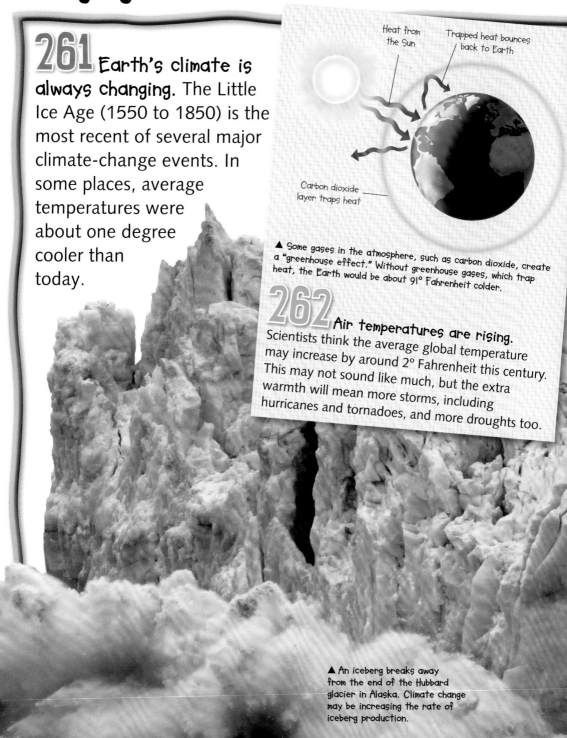

261 **Earth's climate is always changing.** The Little Ice Age (1550 to 1850) is the most recent of several major climate-change events. In some places, average temperatures were about one degree cooler than today.

Heat from the Sun

Trapped heat bounces back to Earth

Carbon dioxide layer traps heat

▲ Some gases in the atmosphere, such as carbon dioxide, create a "greenhouse effect." Without greenhouse gases, which trap heat, the Earth would be about 91° Fahrenheit colder.

262 **Air temperatures are rising.** Scientists think the average global temperature may increase by around 2° Fahrenheit this century. This may not sound like much, but the extra warmth will mean more storms, including hurricanes and tornadoes, and more droughts too.

▲ An iceberg breaks away from the end of the Hubbard glacier in Alaska. Climate change may be increasing the rate of iceberg production.

263 Tree-felling is affecting our weather.

In areas of Southeast Asia and South America, rain forests are being cleared for farming. When the trees are burned, the fires release carbon dioxide—a greenhouse gas that helps to blanket the Earth and keep in the heat. High levels of carbon dioxide raise the temperature too much.

▶ Like all plants, rain forest trees take in carbon dioxide and give out oxygen. As rain forests are destroyed, the amount of carbon dioxide in the atmosphere increases.

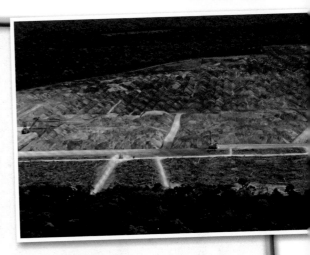

264 Some sea creatures, such as the colorful corals that live mainly in shallow water, are very sensitive to temperature.

As the atmosphere gradually warms up, so does the temperature of the surface water. This causes the coral animals, called polyps, to die, leaving behind their lifeless, stony skeletons.

◀ The death of corals through changes in water temperature is known as "bleaching."

QUIZ

1. When was the Little Ice Age?
2. Where do corals mainly live?
3. What gas is released when trees are burned?

Answers:
1. 1550 to 1850 2. In shallow water 3. Carbon dioxide

265 The long-term effects of climate change are uncertain.

In the short-term it seems very likely that the climate will become more unstable, and that there will be an increase in the number and intensity of extreme weather events. Weather forecasting has always been important, but in the future it will become even more so as we adapt to Earth's changing climate.

SAVING THE EARTH

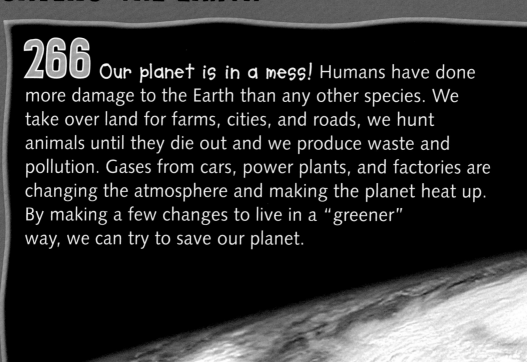

266 **Our planet is in a mess!** Humans have done more damage to the Earth than any other species. We take over land for farms, cities, and roads, we hunt animals until they die out and we produce waste and pollution. Gases from cars, power plants, and factories are changing the atmosphere and making the planet heat up. By making a few changes to live in a "greener" way, we can try to save our planet.

▼ As pollution makes the Earth warm up, more powerful storms form over the sea. This satellite photo shows Hurricane Frances moving over the Caribbean in 2004.

Global warming

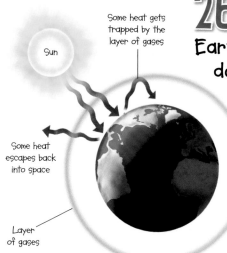

Sun

Some heat gets trapped by the layer of gases

Some heat escapes back into space

Layer of gases

▲ Global warming happens when greenhouse gases collect in the Earth's atmosphere. They let heat from the Sun through, but as it bounces back, it gets trapped close to the Earth, making the planet heat up.

267 Throughout its history, the Earth has warmed up and cooled down. Experts think that today's warming is down to humans— and it's happening faster than normal. Carbon dioxide and methane gases are released into the air as pollution. They are known as greenhouse gases and can stop the Sun's heat escaping from the atmosphere.

268 Global warming tells us that the climate is changing. Weather changes every day—we have hot days and cold days—but on average the climate is warming up. Scientists think that average temperatures have risen by about two degrees Fahrenheit in the last 100 years, and that they will keep rising.

I DON'T BELIEVE IT!

Scientists think that sea levels could rise by three feet by 2100— maybe even more. Three million years ago when the Earth was hotter, the sea was 650 feet higher than today. We could be heading that way again.

269 Warmer temperatures mean wilder weather. Wind happens when air is heated and gets lighter. It rises up and cold air is sucked in to replace it. Rain occurs when heat makes water in rivers and seas turn into vapor in the air. It rises up and forms rain clouds. Warmer temperatures mean more wind, rain, and storms.

KEY

Average area of sea covered by ice from 1980–2000

Predicted area of sea covered by ice for 2080–2100

ARCTIC OCEAN

◀ The ice in the Arctic Ocean is melting so fast that scientists think over half of it could be gone by 2100.

▼ Huge chunks of ice often break off into the sea at Paradise Bay, at the Antarctic.

270 As the Earth heats up, its ice melts.

Vast areas of the Earth are covered in ice. It is found around the North and South Poles, and on high mountains. Now, because of global warming, more and more of this ice is melting. It turns into water and flows into the sea. Also, as the water gets warmer, it expands (gets bigger) and the sea takes up more space, making sea levels rise.

▶ Polar bears depend on large chunks of ice to hunt and rest on. Melting ice in the Arctic is making life much harder for them.

Energy crisis

271
We pump greenhouse gases into the atmosphere because we burn fuels to make energy. Cars, planes, and trains run on fuel, and we also burn it in power plants to produce electricity. The main fuels—coal, oil, and gas—are called fossil fuels because they formed underground over millions of years.

▶ Oil and natural gas formed from the remains of tiny prehistoric sea creatures that collected on the seabed. Layers of rock built up on top and squashed them. Over time, they became underground stores of oil, with pockets of gas above.

272
Fossil fuels are running out. Because they take so long to form, we are using up fossil fuels much faster than they can be replaced. Eventually, they will become so rare that it will be too expensive to find them. Experts think this will happen before the end of the 21st century.

Oil platform drilling for oil and gas

Hard rock layer

Gas

Oil

Oil and gas move upward through soft rock layers until reaching a hard rock layer

The layer of dead sea creatures is crushed by rock that forms above, and turns into oil and gas

Tiny sea creatures die and sink to the seabed

QUIZ
Which of these things are used to supply electricity?
A. Burning coal B. Wind
C. The flow of rivers
D. Hamsters on wheels E. Sunshine
F. The energy of earthquakes

Answers:
A, B, C, and E. Hamsters could turn tiny turbines, but would make very little electricity. Earthquakes contain vast amounts of energy, but we have not found a way to harness it.

273
One thing we can do is find other fuels. Besides fossil fuels, we can burn fuels that come from plants. For example, the rapeseed plant contains oil that can be burned in vehicle engines. However, burning these fuels still releases greenhouse gases.

274
Nuclear power is another kind of energy. By splitting apart atoms—the tiny units that all materials are made of—energy is released, which can be turned into electricity. However, producing this energy creates toxic waste that can make people ill, and may be accidentally released into the air. Safer ways to use nuclear power are being researched.

▲ The Grand Coulee Dam in Washington, US, holds back a river, creating a lake, or reservoir. Water is let through the dam to turn turbines, which create electricity.

275
Lots of energy is produced without burning anything. Hydroelectric power plants use the pushing power of flowing rivers to turn turbines. Hydroelectricity is a renewable, or green, energy source—it doesn't use anything up or cause pollution. Scientists are also working on ways to turn the movement of waves and tides into usable energy.

276
The wind and the Sun are great renewable sources of energy, too. Wind turbines turn generators, which convert the "turning movement" into electricity. Solar panels work by collecting sunlight and turning it into an electrical current.

◀ Solar panels are made of materials that soak up sunlight and turn its energy into a flow of electricity.

Rotor blade

▲ Modern wind turbines usually have three blades, which spin around at speed in high winds.

On the move

277 **Cars release a lot of greenhouse gases.** No one had a car 200 years ago. Now, there are around 500 million cars in the world and most are used daily. Cars burn gasoline or diesel, which are made from oil—a fossil fuel. We can reduce greenhouse gases and slow down global warming by using cars less.

Carbon dioxide (CO_2)

Nitrogen dioxide (NO_2)

Sulfur dioxide (SO_2)

▲ Car exhaust fumes contain harmful, polluting gases, including sulfur dioxide, nitrogen dioxide, and carbon dioxide, which are poisonous to humans.

▼ In many cities, there are so many cars that they cause big traffic jams. They move slowly with their engines running, churning out even more pollution.

278 **Public transport is made up of buses, trams, and trains that everyone can use.** It's a greener way to travel than by car. Buses can carry 60 or 70 people at once and trains can carry several hundred. They still burn fuel, but release much less greenhouse gases per person.

COUNT YOUR STEPS

Besides saving on greenhouse gases, walking is great exercise and helps you stay healthy. Try counting your steps for one whole day. How many can you do—3,000, 5,000, or even 10,000?

279
Planes fly long distances at high speeds, giving out tons of greenhouse gases on each journey. A return flight from the UK to the US releases more carbon dioxide than a car does in one year. Where you can, travel by boat or train for shorter jouneys.

▲ Maglev trains use magnets to hover above the rails. The magnetic force propels the train forward, rather than a gasoline or diesel-burning engine.

▲ Cyclists in Beijing, China, enjoy World Car-Free Day. This was organized to help reduce pollution.

◄ This graph shows the world's top ten producers of carbon dioxide pollution (carbon dioxide is a major greenhouse gas). These figures are based on emissions in 2015.

CO_2 emissions (millions of tons)

11,000
10,000
9000
8000
7000
6000
5000
4000
3000
2000
1000
0

China   USA   India   Russia   Japan   Germany   Iran   South Korea   Canada   Saudi Arabia

280
The greenest way to get around is to walk. For short journeys, walk instead of going by car. Inside buildings, use the stairs instead of taking elevators and escalators. Cycling is good, too. A bicycle doesn't burn any fuels, it just uses the power of your legs.

281
Long ago, before engines and turbines were invented, transport worked differently. Boats had sails or oars and were driven by wind or human power, and carts and carriages were pulled by animals. As fossil fuels run out, we may see some old means of transport coming back.

Save energy at home

282 Saving electricity at home reduces pollution. Most electricity we use is produced from burning fossil fuels. By using less of it, we can cut greenhouse gas emissions. Always turn off lights, TVs, computers, and other electrical devices when not in use. Low-energy light bulbs are a good idea, too. They use less power and last longer.

▼ Washing hung outside dries in the heat of the Sun. This saves on electricity and fossil fuels.

FIVE ENERGY-SAVING TIPS

Turn appliances off properly
Switch appliances off at the "off" switch or at the plug. Appliances left in standby mode still use electricity.

Make sure your cooking pots have lids on
This saves energy by reducing cooking time.

Don't overfill your kettle
Just boil the amount of water that you need—this will save energy.

Buy fresh foods instead of frozen
Much more energy is used to produce frozen foods, so buy fresh when you can.

Turn down your heating by one degree
You won't really notice the difference, and you could save around 10 percent off your energy bill.

284 We invent all kinds of electrical gadgets to do things for us, but do we really need them? You can save energy by sweeping the floor instead of using a vacuum cleaner every time. Use your hands to make bread, instead of a food processor. Avoid electrical can openers, knives, and other power-hungry gadgets.

283 Your washing can be green as well as clean! Tumble dryers dry quickly, but they use lots of electricity. In summer, peg your clothes out on a washing line in the garden. In winter, hang them on a rack close to a radiator. You can save even more energy by washing clothes at a lower temperature, such as 80°F.

I DON'T BELIEVE IT!

Only 10 percent of the electricity used by an old-style light bulb is turned into light. The rest turns into wasted heat, which also makes it burn out quicker.

285

Solar panels are a green way to power a home. They work the same way that solar-powered calculators do— they can change sunlight into electricity straight away. If a home produces more electricity than it needs, it can sell some back to the local energy provider.

▼ Solar panels are often made of silicon. When sunlight hits the silicon, electrical charges can flow as an electrical current.

▲ Solar panels can be installed on rooftops to provide power for homes.

Sunlight

Sunlight

Wires carry the flow of electricity to appliances, such as lights

Solar panel

▼ Growing turf on the roof is a good way to insulate a house to prevent heat from escaping and being wasted. The grass uses up CO_2 and makes oxygen, too.

286

Turn down the heating in your house and keep warm in other ways! If you're cold put on an extra layer of clothing, or wrap up warm under a blanket. You will also save energy if your home has insulation in the walls and roof, and double-glazed windows.

Green shopping

287 Most people buy something from a shop every day. Items such as food, clothes, and furniture take a lot of energy to grow, manufacture, and then transport to the shops. By doing some smart shopping, you can save some of that energy.

▲ Old plastic bags fill up landfill sites and take hundreds of years to rot away. They can also harm wildlife and farm animals.

▶ Bags made from cloth can be used over and over again.

QUIZ

1. Which kind of shopping bag is greenest—plastic, paper, or cloth?

2. Which costs more—bottled water or tap water?

3. What is vintage clothing?

Answers:
1. A reusable cloth bag
2. Bottled water
3. Second-hand clothes

288 Say no to plastic bags! Plastic bags are made from oil—a fossil fuel—and it takes energy to make them. However, we often use them once then throw them away, which creates trash and pollution. When you go shopping take a reusable bag made from cloth, or reuse old plastic bags so that you don't have to use new ones.

289 How far has your food traveled? The distance food has been transported is called "food miles." You can reduce food miles by shopping at farm stores and local markets. In grocery stores, look at packages to find food that was produced nearby. Food that has traveled far is greener if it came by boat, and not by plane.

▲ On the island of Saint Vincent in the Caribbean, people buy bananas that have been grown locally. Bananas grown here are also shipped to other countries—a much greener way to transport than by plane.

290 More and more people are buying bottled water. Water is heavy and a lot of fuel is needed to transport it long distances. The plastic bottles create waste and cause pollution, too. It's greener to use clean, pure water from the tap at home.

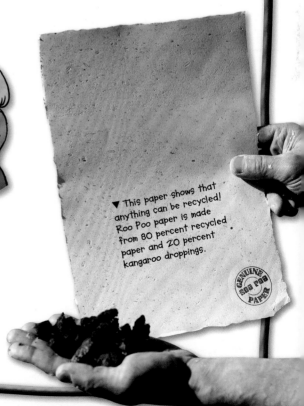

▼ This paper shows that anything can be recycled! Roo Poo paper is made from 80 percent recycled paper and 20 percent kangaroo droppings.

GENUINE ROO POO PAPER

291 Buying second-hand goods is a great way to save energy. When you buy second-hand clothes, furniture, or books nothing new has to be made in a factory. Antique furniture and vintage clothes are often better quality than new things and more individual, too.

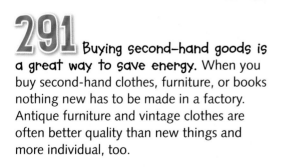

Reduce, reuse, recycle

292 **Most of us buy more than we need.** We want the latest clothes, toys, and cars even though we may not need them—this is called consumerism. Reduce, reuse, and recycle is a good way to remember what we can do to reduce the amount of things we buy.

293 **To start with, reduce your shopping.** Do you or your family ever buy things that don't end up getting used? Next time, think before you buy—be sure that you are going to use it. Buying less means less things have to be made, transported, and thrown away. It saves money, too!

Empty glass bottles go into a recycling bin.

▶ Recycling materials greatly reduces the amount of energy needed to make new products. This graph shows how much energy is saved in making new products using recycled materials, rather than raw materials.

Aluminum	95 percent
Plastics	70 percent
Steel	60 percent
Newspaper	40 percent
Glass	40 percent

0   20   40   60   80   100

Percentage of energy saved by recycling

294 **Recycling means that materials can be made into new things instead of thrown away.** This saves energy and makes less waste. Paper, cardboard, food cans, glass, and some plastics can all be recycled. Some local councils collect them, or you can take them to a recycling collection point.

The bottles are collected from the bin and transported to a glass recycling plant.

The old, broken glass is cleaned and melted down with other substances.

295 We live in a "throwaway society." We are used to disposable things that get used once, then go in the trash. When something breaks, it's easy to get another, but making and transporting these new things uses up raw materials, and creates pollution. Reuse some of the things you throw away —mend clothes by sewing on a new button, pocket, or patch and use empty food containers to store things in.

I DON'T BELIEVE IT!

Many things we buy are built to break easily. This is called "built-in obsolescence." Manufacturers hope that when your things break, you'll buy new ones from them.

▼ These shopping bags have been made from old, recycled food sacks. They save on raw materials and cut down on plastic bags.

296 If you can't reuse something yourself, maybe someone else can. Give old clothes, furniture, books, and toys to charity, or sell them at a yard sale or a rummage sale at school.

The bottles are sold and used, and can then be recycled again.

▼ Recycled glass is used in road surfaces, concrete production, and a finely ground glass is used to fill golf bunkers. New bottles and jars are also made from recycled glass.

The bottles are filled with drinks and labeled.

The liquid glass is blow molded (blown with air) into new bottles.

Green machines

297 As well as using machines less, we can use greener ones. Cars, computers, and electrical appliances don't have to use lots of energy. Scientists are working on greener versions that use less electricity or fuel—or even none at all.

298 When hydrogen gas burns, it doesn't release any greenhouse gases—just water. Today, some cars run on hydrogen and create no pollution. However, making the hydrogen for them to run on uses up electricity, and in turn fossil fuels. As fossil fuels run out and renewable energy sources take over, hydrogen cars may become common.

▼ A hydrogen-powered car and a hydrogen fuel station show what more of us could be using in the future.

Hydrogen
Fuel station Vetnisstöð

HYDROGEN
GM
GM FUEL CELL TECHNOLOGY

HYDROGEN3

IN EMERGENCY, CALL
112
HEYDARLINAN

299
You might have traveled on an electric train or bus before. Instead of burning fuel, they run on electricity supplied from a large, onboard battery or overhead cables. This means less air pollution in city centers.

▲ Trams like this can be found in many cities around the world. They work by collecting electricity from overhead wires or cables.

300
Did you know that "white goods" can be green? White goods are refrigerators, washing machines, dishwashers, and other kitchen appliances. New ones have a rating showing how green they are. The greenest ones use the least energy and supplies such as water. Now you can choose the best ones for the planet.

▶ This solar-powered cell phone charger uses solar panels to turn sunlight into an electricity supply.

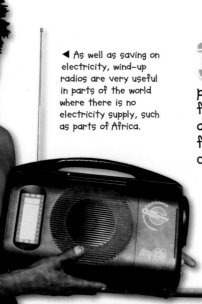

◀ As well as saving on electricity, wind-up radios are very useful in parts of the world where there is no electricity supply, such as parts of Africa.

301
Wind-up power was once used for toys, but now there are wind-up radios, flashlights, and cell phone chargers. The handle is wound and the energy from this movement is turned into an electricity supply inside the machine. Wind-up machines save on fossil fuels and reduce greenhouse gases.

Science solutions

▼ An artist's impression of a space shield that could be used to shade the Earth from the Sun.

302 **Using less energy is one way to slow down global warming, but there might be others, too.** Scientists are coming up with all kinds of space-age and hi-tech solutions that could help the Earth to cool down again.

303 **Maybe we could shade the Earth to cool it down.** Scientists have lots of ideas about how to do this. Some of these include launching huge mirrors into space to reflect the Sun's light and heat away, or filling the atmosphere with tiny particles to blot out the Sun. Another is to spread out a fine mesh, like a giant sheet, into space to make a sunshade. So far, all of these ideas are far too expensive to try.

I DON'T BELIEVE IT!

In a single day a cow can give out 110 gallons of methane gas. That's enough to fill more than 100 party balloons!

304

Instead of greenhouse gases filling the air, we could soak them up. Plants naturally take in carbon dioxide (CO_2)—a greenhouse gas—so planting lots of trees helps to slow global warming. Scientists are also trying to develop special types of algae (tiny plants) that can soak up even more greenhouse gases.

▶ A huge cloud of green algae can be seen near the shore of Lake Tahoe, US. Algae is made up of millions of tiny plants. There is so much algae in the world that it soaks up a lot of the world's carbon dioxide.

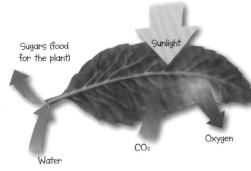

Sugars (food for the plant)

Sunlight

Oxygen

CO_2

Water

▲ Plants make food using sunlight, by a process called photosynthesis. They use up carbon dioxide and give out oxygen.

305

We could catch greenhouse gases before they escape into the air. There are already devices that can do this, which capture carbon dioxide from power stations and factory chimneys. Once it is caught, the gas needs to be stored safely. Scientists are looking at ways of storing carbon dioxide, or changing it into something harmless.

▼ A special foam wrapping is unrolled over the Tortin glacier in Switzerland to stop it melting.

306

As they digest grass, cows and other grazing animals pass a lot of wind! This gas contains methane—a greenhouse gas. Besides burning fuels, this is one of the biggest causes of global warming. Scientists are experimenting with feeding cows different foods to reduce the amount of methane.

Pollution problems

307 **Pollution means dirt, waste, and other substances that damage our surroundings.** Our farms and factories often release harmful chemicals into rivers and lakes, and cars, trucks, and other road vehicles give out poisonous, polluting gases. Trash and garbage are pollution, too.

▼ A thick layer of smog hangs over the city of Bangkok, the capital of Thailand.

308 **Humans make waste— when we go to the toilet.** The waste and water from our toilets is called sewage. This usually ends up at sewage treatment plant where we process it to make it safe, but in some places sewage flows straight into rivers or the sea. It is dirty and can contain deadly germs.

309 **Pollution can harm our health.** Smog is a mixture of smoke from factories and motor vehicles, and fog, and it collects over some cities. It makes it harder to breathe, worsening illnesses such as asthma.

◀ People in Kuala Lumpur, the capital of Malaysia, wear masks to avoid breathing in smog.

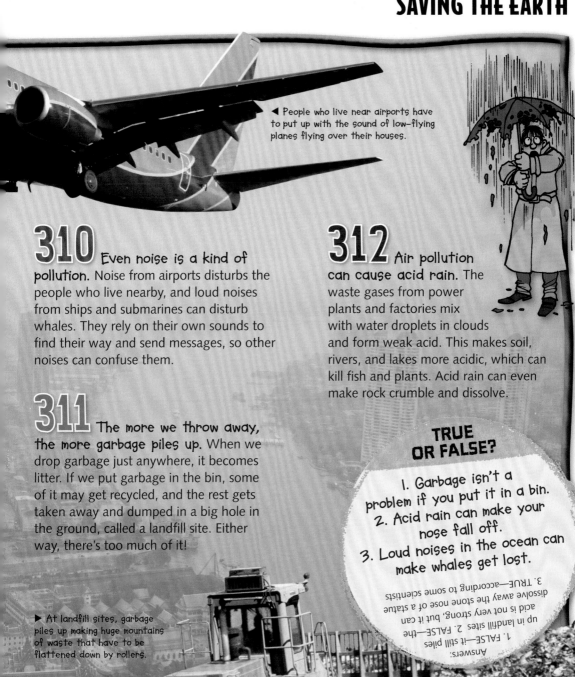

◀ People who live near airports have to put up with the sound of low-flying planes flying over their houses.

310
Even noise is a kind of pollution. Noise from airports disturbs the people who live nearby, and loud noises from ships and submarines can disturb whales. They rely on their own sounds to find their way and send messages, so other noises can confuse them.

311
The more we throw away, the more garbage piles up. When we drop garbage just anywhere, it becomes litter. If we put garbage in the bin, some of it may get recycled, and the rest gets taken away and dumped in a big hole in the ground, called a landfill site. Either way, there's too much of it!

▶ At landfill sites, garbage piles up making huge mountains of waste that have to be flattened down by rollers.

312
Air pollution can cause acid rain. The waste gases from power plants and factories mix with water droplets in clouds and form weak acid. This makes soil, rivers, and lakes more acidic, which can kill fish and plants. Acid rain can even make rock crumble and dissolve.

TRUE OR FALSE?

1. Garbage isn't a problem if you put it in a bin.
2. Acid rain can make your nose fall off.
3. Loud noises in the ocean can make whales get lost.

Answers:
1. FALSE—it still piles up in landfill sites 2. FALSE—the acid is not very strong, but it can dissolve away the stone nose of a statue 3. TRUE—according to some scientists

Litter and garbage

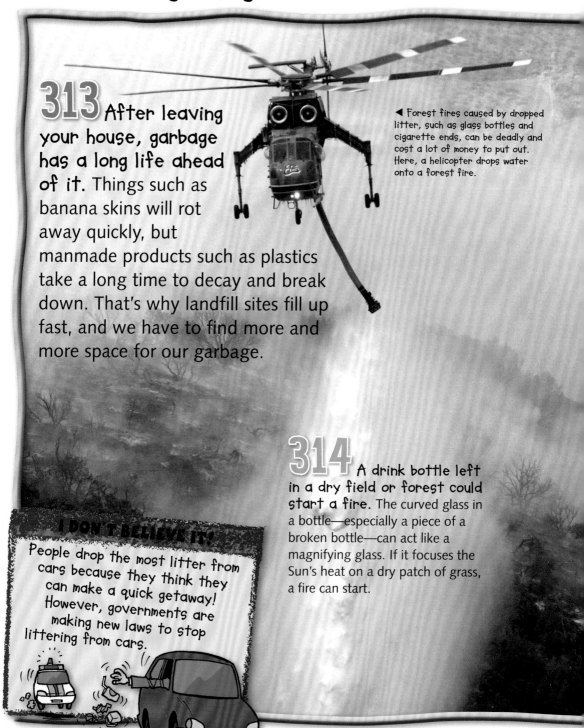

313 After leaving your house, garbage has a long life ahead of it. Things such as banana skins will rot away quickly, but manmade products such as plastics take a long time to decay and break down. That's why landfill sites fill up fast, and we have to find more and more space for our garbage.

◀ Forest fires caused by dropped litter, such as glass bottles and cigarette ends, can be deadly and cost a lot of money to put out. Here, a helicopter drops water onto a forest fire.

314 A drink bottle left in a dry field or forest could start a fire. The curved glass in a bottle—especially a piece of a broken bottle—can act like a magnifying glass. If it focuses the Sun's heat on a dry patch of grass, a fire can start.

I DON'T BELIEVE IT!

People drop the most litter from cars because they think they can make a quick getaway! However, governments are making new laws to stop littering from cars.

▶ Leaving your junk in a public place is illegal. Mattresses, tires and shopping carts are often dumped in the countryside.

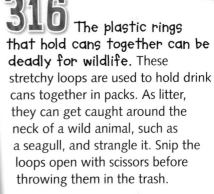

315
Some people treat the countryside and other public places as a dumping ground. Big items, such as mattresses, sofas, and shopping carts, are sometimes dumped on roadsides or in rivers. Besides looking a mess, these things can release poisons as they rot away.

316
The plastic rings that hold cans together can be deadly for wildlife. These stretchy loops are used to hold drink cans together in packs. As litter, they can get caught around the neck of a wild animal, such as a seagull, and strangle it. Snip the loops open with scissors before throwing them in the trash.

▲ Ducks struggle through a pond polluted with plastic bottles.

▼ Fishing nets left on beaches can endanger wildlife. This one has become tangled around a sea lion's neck.

317
Fishing weights and lines left near rivers and lakes can choke or strangle water wildlife. Weights sometimes contain lead and this can poison water birds, such as swans. People who go fishing should make sure they never leave any of their equipment behind.

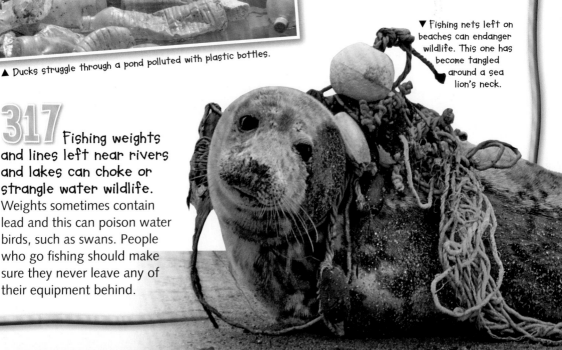

Reducing waste

318 There are lots of things you can do to reduce waste. When you throw something away, think if it could be recycled or reused instead. Avoid buying things that will have to be thrown away after one use.

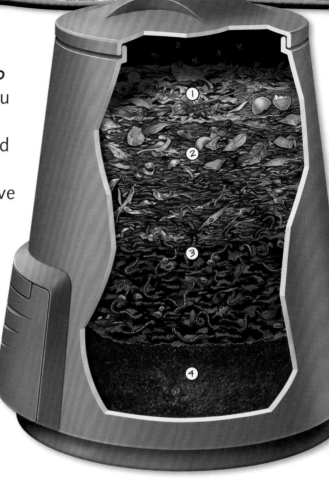

▲ You can buy a specially made compost bin to make compost in, like this one.

MAKE SOME COMPOST

Make a heap of plant waste, fruit and vegetable skins, and grass cuttings in a corner of your garden. It takes a few months to turn into compost. To help it along, mix it around and dig it over with a garden fork. When the compost is ready, you can use it for potting plants or add it to soil in your yard.

319 Instead of throwing away fruit and vegetable peelings, turn them into compost. When your peelings rot down, they turn into a rich, fertile soil that's great for your yard. All you need is a space outside where you can pile up your waste for composting, or you can get a special compost bin.

The composting process

① Waste, including fruit and vegetable peelings, teabags, leaves, and eggshells, goes in the top.

② Tiny organisms called microbes start to break down the waste, which makes it heat up.

③ Insects help to break it down even more and worms help air to get into the compost.

④ The compost is brown and moist and should smell earthy.

320 Millions of disposable batteries end up in landfill sites every year. They take a long time to decay and when they do, they release harmful chemicals. Rechargeable batteries can be refilled with energy from the mains and reused many times.

322 Lots of the things we buy come wrapped up several times over. We take them home, unwrap them, and throw the packaging away. Choose products with less packaging, or none at all.

321 Reduce your waste—pick reusables, not disposables. Baby wipes and disposable diapers, cups, and cooking trays are all things that we use once, then throw away. It's greener to use reuseables, such as washable baking trays, cloth dish towels, and washable diapers.

▼ Much of our garbage is made up of pointless packaging that we don't really need.

TIME TO DECOMPOSE

Fruit and vegetables	2 days to 6 months
Newspaper	6 months
Drink cans	100 to 500 years
Disposable diapers	200 to 500 years
Plastic bags	450 years
Plastic bottles	100 to 1,000 years +

Cutting pollution

323 **Big companies need to cut the pollution they produce.** There are laws to ban them dumping toxic chemicals and to limit dangerous waste gases, but they're not yet tough enough to make a big difference. Pressure groups such as Greenpeace are fighting for stronger, better laws.

▲ This tractor is spraying chemicals onto crops to kill pests and weeds. When it rains the chemicals wash into rivers and can harm wildlife.

324 Weedkillers and insect sprays kill unwanted plants and bugs in the garden. However, because they are poisonous they can kill other wildlife too, and cause pollution. It's greener to pull up weeds and pick off pests instead.

▼ This tractor is using a different method—cutting back weeds between the crops, instead of spraying them. This keeps the environment cleaner.

325 Cleaning your house can make the planet dirty! Strong cleaning chemicals that are washed down the sink can end up in water supplies. Try to use less of them, or use natural, homemade alternatives. A mixture of water and vinegar is great for cleaning windows.

▶ Some companies are now making reusable washing balls that clean clothes without using any detergent.

326 Paint, paint stripper, and varnish contain toxic chemicals. These chemicals don't break down naturally when they are poured away, which results in pollution. If you can, save them to use again, or see if your local council will collect them for reusing (some councils do this).

327 Shampoo, face creams, and makeup are full of polluting chemicals. Pick greener products that contain natural ingredients. You can even use everyday ingredients, such as olive oil, to make your own skin treatments.

▲ Soap nuts are berries of the soapberry tree. They contain a natural, soapy chemical that can be used to wash clothes.

MAKE A FOOT SOAK

Mix together:
1 tablespoon of fine oatmeal
1 tablespoon of skim milk powder
1 teaspoonful of dried rosemary

Spoon the mixture into an old, clean sock and tie a knot at the top. Leave the sock in a bowl of warm water for a few minutes, then soak your feet in the water for 20 minutes.

Wildlife in danger

328 Since humans have existed on Earth, many living things have been destroyed. To make space for cities, farms, and roads, people have taken over wild areas, and plants and animals have lost their natural homes, or habitats. This is called habitat loss and it is the main reason why wildlife is in danger.

▲ Wild animals, such as crocodiles, are still killed for their skins to make items such as handbags and rugs.

▼ This bird is covered in oil spilt from an oil tanker (a ship that carries oil). If birds like this aren't cleaned, they will die.

329 Toxic waste, oil spills, and pesticides can be deadly for wildlife. In the 1950s, a chemical called DDT was used to kill insects on crops, but it affected other animals including wild birds. It made them lay eggs with very thin shells that cracked easily. The birds began to die out as they could not have chicks.

330
Wild plants and animals suffer when we exploit them—use them to meet our needs. Humans hunt wild animals for their skins, meat, and other body parts, such as ivory from elephants' tusks. Some people steal wild plants, too. If too many are taken, their numbers fall fast.

◀ These nature reserve wardens in Dzanga–Ndoki National Park in the Central African Republic have caught some poachers hunting protected animals.

QUIZ

What do these words mean?
1. Extinct   2. Species
3. Endangered   4. Habitat

Answers:
1. Died out and no longer existing. 2. A particular type of living thing. 3. In danger of becoming extinct. 4. The surroundings where a plant or animal lives

331
Human activities have wiped out some species, or types, of living things. When a species no longer exists, it is said to be extinct. The great auk—a large-beaked, black-and-white sea bird —became extinct in the 1850s due to hunting by humans. Many other species are now close to extinction, including the tiger and mountain gorilla.

▼ The orangutan— a type of ape—is an extremely threatened species, and one of our closest animal cousins.

332
When a creature is in danger of becoming extinct, we call it threatened. Severely threatened species are known as endangered. These labels help to teach people about the dangers to wildlife. They also help us to make laws to try to protect these species from hunters and collectors.

Saving habitats

333 To save wildlife, we need to save habitats. Humans are taking up more and more space and if we don't slow down, there'll be no wild, natural land left. We need to leave plenty of natural areas for wildlife to live in.

▲ These penguins live in Antarctica. Their habitat is ice and freezing water and it could be affected by global warming.

334 One hundred years ago, people went on safari to hunt animals. Today, more tourists go to watch wild animals and plants in their natural habitat—this is called ecotourism and it helps wildlife. Local people can make enough money from tourism, so they don't need to hunt. However, ecotourism can disturb wildlife, so tourists have to take care where they go.

▶ Tourists in a jeep approach a pride of lions in a nature reserve in South Africa.

335 Nature reserves and national parks are safe homes for wildlife. The land is kept wild and unspoiled to preserve natural habitats. There are also guards or wardens to protect the wildlife and watch out for hunters.

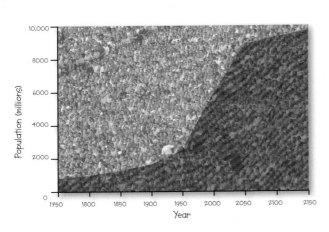

Population (millions) vs Year graph with Y-axis from 0 to 10,000 and X-axis from 1750 to 2150.

▲ As the human population continues to rise, more and more wild, natural land is being taken over.

336 *It can be hard for humans to preserve habitats because we need space too.* There are nearly 8 billion (8,000,000,000) humans on Earth today. Experts think this will rise to at least 9 billion. Some countries have laws to limit the number of children people are allowed to have to try to control the population.

▼ A diver explores a coral reef. The corals are home to many species of fish, crabs, and shellfish.

337 *You can help to keep habitats safe.* In the countryside, don't take stones, shells, or flowers. Visit nature reserves—your money helps to run them. Don't buy souvenirs made of coral, or other animals or plants, as this encourages hunting and habitat destruction.

I DON'T BELIEVE IT!

The river Thames in London, UK has just 10 percent of the pollution it had in the 1950s because of pollution prevention, and is home to over 100 species of fish.

In the garden

338 If you have a grassy area at home or at school, you could make it into a safe place for wildlife to live. Parks are parts of towns and cities that can stay wild. They can be a good habitat for many species of small animals and wild plants.

◀ An insect box provides a home for creatures, such as bees and ladybugs.

▼ Hedgehogs like hiding under leaves. If you have hedgehogs in your garden, don't give them milk as it's bad for them, but try meat scraps, berries, and grated cheese instead.

339 Wild creatures love a messy garden. If gardens are always tidy there is nowhere for animals to hide. Leave parts of your backyard untidy and overgrown—let grass and weeds grow and don't clear up piles of leaves. These areas provide shelter and homes for spiders, beetles, birds, and small mammals.

FOOD FOR BIRDS

Here are some snacks to try putting out for garden birds:
Grated hard cheese
Raisins
Sunflower seeds or other seeds
Chopped or crushed nuts
Meat scraps
Fresh, chopped coconut

Avoid putting out dry or salty food, such as stale bread or salted nuts, as it's bad for birds.

340 You can help wild birds by feeding them. Feed birds in winter—there are fewer berries and insects for them to eat at this time of year. Put up a bird table, or hang bird feeders from trees in your garden.

▲ Butterflies such as tortoiseshells like to feed on the flowers of a buddleia bush.

◄ A coal tit and a red squirrel are helping themselves to nuts from this bird feeder.

341 Bees and butterflies feed on nectar—a sweet juice found inside flowers. A garden full of flowers will provide lots of food for insects. They especially like sunflowers, lavender, and buddleia bushes.

▶ Sunflowers are great for wildlife. They provide nectar for insects and nutritious seeds for birds.

342 Thick, thorny bushes are brilliant for birds. Some bushes, such as brambles and hawthorns, provide berries that birds like to eat. Thick, tangled bushes also make safe places for birds to build their nests or hide from animals, such as pet cats.

Saving species

343 Goods made from threatened wildlife species can be bought around the world. Although there are laws to protect plants and animals, they are often broken. It's best not to buy anything that might come from a threatened species, such as ivory, skins, horns, or bones.

◄ Parrots are sometimes stolen from the wild as chicks and sold as pets.

345 You or your class could sponsor an endangered animal, such as a tiger. You pay a small fee that goes toward caring for the animal and running the zoo or reserve where it lives. In return, you'll get letters or emails about your animal's progress. Zoos and wildlife organizations can help you to do this.

344 Exotic pets can be exciting, but they are sometimes stolen from the wild. Avoid having an unusual pet such as a rare lizard or parrot. It could be a threatened species that has been taken away from its natural habitat.

◀ A Greenpeace ship (far left) encounters a whaling ship, the Nisshin Maru, in the Antarctic Ocean. Some countries still hunt whales, but campaigning groups such as Greenpeace are trying to stop it.

I DON'T BELIEVE IT!

Millions of sharks, including threatened species, are hunted every year to make shark's fin soup. The soup is an expensive delicacy in China.

346 People still hunt threatened species, even though it's illegal. Many people in the world are very poor and some can't resist hunting a threatened tiger to sell its skin, or a shark to sell its fins. Governments need to try to reduce poverty, to help wildlife as well as people.

▼ In China, giant pandas are being bred successfully on wildlife reserves. These are just some of the new babies born in recent years.

347 To help endangered animals, visit your nearest zoo. Most zoos have captive breeding programs. These help endangered animals to have babies to increase their numbers. Some can then be released back into the wild.

Forests and farms

348
Every year, nearly 30 million acres of forests are logged (cut down). That's an area the size of the country of Malawi in Africa, or the US state of Pennsylvania. Trees do grow again, but we are cutting forests down much faster than they can grow back.

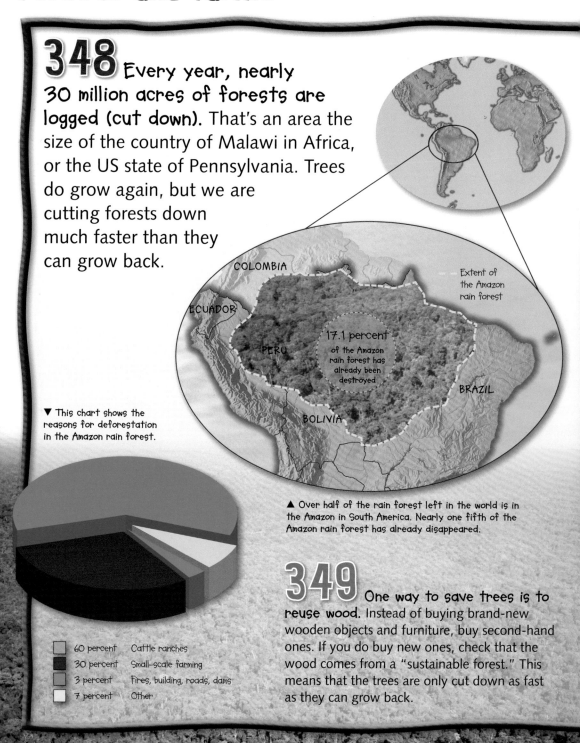

COLOMBIA

ECUADOR

PERU

17.1 percent
of the Amazon rain forest has already been destroyed

BOLIVIA

BRAZIL

Extent of the Amazon rain forest

▼ This chart shows the reasons for deforestation in the Amazon rain forest.

▲ Over half of the rain forest left in the world is in the Amazon in South America. Nearly one fifth of the Amazon rain forest has already disappeared.

60 percent	Cattle ranches
30 percent	Small-scale farming
3 percent	Fires, building, roads, dams
7 percent	Other

349
One way to save trees is to reuse wood. Instead of buying brand-new wooden objects and furniture, buy second-hand ones. If you do buy new ones, check that the wood comes from a "sustainable forest." This means that the trees are only cut down as fast as they can grow back.

350 Farms take up almost 40 percent of the Earth's land. We need farms to provide us with food—to grow crops and keep animals on—but they have a big impact on the Earth. Most farmland is devoted to one type of crop or animal, so many types of wildlife that live there lose their homes.

▲ Large areas of rain forest in Indonesia and Malaysia have been cut down to make way for oil palm tree plantations. The fruits of the oil palm are harvested for their oil, which can be found in one in three supermarket products.

351 Organic farming can be a greener way to farm. It doesn't use artificial chemicals, such as pesticides and fertilizers, which means it is good for wildlife and the soil. If you buy organic food and other products, you help to keep the Earth cleaner.

352 Buying nuts can help save the rain forests. Some products, such as brazil nuts, grow on rain forest trees. By buying them, you are helping farmers to keep rain forests alive, instead of cutting them down to grow other crops.

▶ As most nuts grow on trees, they are one crop that can be grown without cutting trees down.

Seas and coasts

353 Seas and oceans cover the biggest part of the Earth's surface— nearly three-quarters of it! Pollution, global warming, and fishing have a huge effect on the sea and its wildlife.

354 Pollution from farms, factories, and houses often flows into rivers and ends up in the sea. Tiny sea plants and animals absorb the chemicals. When they are eaten by larger sea creatures, the polluting chemicals are passed on from one animal to the next. Many large sea creatures, such as sharks and polar bears, have been found to have a lot of toxic chemicals in their bodies.

355 Coastal areas are in trouble because of rising sea levels. As the sea rises, tides, tsunamis, and storm waves can reach further inland. If the sea rises much more, it could put many coastal cities underwater. The danger of the sea flooding the land is one of the biggest reasons to try to slow global warming down.

◀ In Thailand, signs on beaches and streets give warnings and provide evacuation directions to be used in the event of a tsunami. Thailand is one of the countries that was devastated by the tsunami that struck on December 26, 2004.

356 For thousands of years, humans have hunted fish. Today, we are catching so many fish that some types are in danger of disappearing—this is called overfishing. To try to stop it, there are laws to give fishing boats a quota, or limit, on how many fish they can catch.

▼ Low-lying islands, such as this one in Fiji, are in danger of disappearing as sea levels rise.

▶ Cod is one type of fish that has been overfished in some parts of the world.

357 There's precious treasure in the seabed. It contains oil—a fossil fuel—and many other useful minerals. However, drilling and digging into the seabed damages wildlife and sea habitats, such as coral reefs. Governments are starting to set up nature reserves in the sea, as well as on land. In these areas, no mining or drilling is allowed.

◀ Oil rigs such as this one are built around a giant drill that bores into the seabed to extract oil.

Water resources

358 The world is using too much water.

In many places, water is being pumped out of lakes, rivers, and underground wells faster than rain can replace it. As the human population grows, so will the need for water.

▼ Most of the world's freshwater is frozen! The figures below show where the fresh water is found.

Ice caps and glaciers
77.2 percent

Ground water
22.26 percent

Rivers and lakes
0.32 percent

Soil
0.18 percent

Atmosphere
0.04 percent

359 Global warming is causing huge water problems.

Some areas are getting more rain and floods, as hotter temperatures lead to more clouds and storms. Floods often pollute water supplies. Other places are becoming hotter and drier, leading to droughts. Either way, global warming is leading to water shortages.

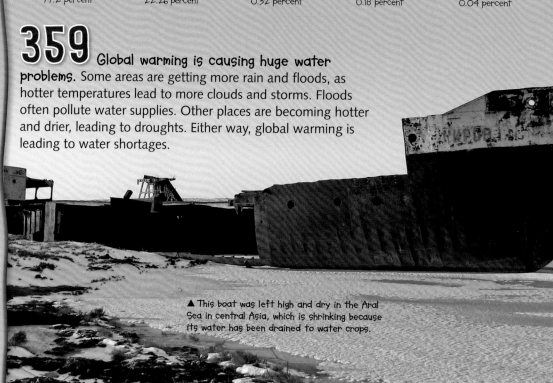

▲ This boat was left high and dry in the Aral Sea in central Asia, which is shrinking because its water has been drained to water crops.

▲ Young women have to lift water deep from a village well in Niger, West Africa.

360 In some countries, drinking water comes from the sea. Seawater is much too salty to drink, but in dry countries, such as Kuwait, they have factories called desalination plants. They take the salt out of seawater to make it fit to drink. However, this process uses up lots of energy and is not a long-term solution.

361 Having a green garden saves water! Many people pave their gardens over for a patio, but rain flows straight off the hard surface and can lead to floods. If gardens are kept as soil and plants, rain soaks into the ground and keeps water supplies topped up.

▼ An aerial view of a desalination plant in Kuwait.

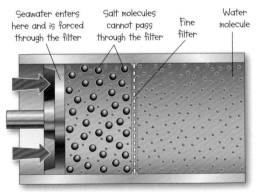

Seawater enters here and is forced through the filter

Salt molecules cannot pass through the filter

Fine filter

Water molecule

▲ The salt is removed from seawater by pushing it through a very fine filter, making it drinkable. This process is called reverse osmosis.

The environment around us

362 The word environment means the place that surrounds us. Planet Earth and all the habitats on it make up our environment. That's why being green is sometimes called environmentalism.

363 As this book shows, the Earth is changing too fast. To be green, and to care for the environment, we need to change the Earth as little as possible. We must reduce the litter, pollution, and greenhouse gases that we produce. At the same time we must take less away from it.

▶ We need to let as much of the Earth as possible stay in its natural state, such as this beautiful forest in Borneo.

TURN YOUR SCHOOL GREEN

One thing you can do to help save the Earth is persuade your school to go green (or greener).

Here are some ideas:
- Arrange a recycling roster to collect waste paper from all the classrooms and offices.
- Make posters to put up in the toilets to remind people to save water.
- If there's space, set up a school wildlife area and compost heap—persuade the kitchen staff to compost food leftovers.

364
Being green is a job for everyone. At home, switching off lights and saving water helps to save the Earth. Towns, communities, and businesses can help, too, by arranging recycling collections, or banning plastic bags. Governments are already starting to pass laws to limit things such as pollution, logging, and overfishing.

365
Planet Earth is the only home we have. It's also the only home for wild animals and plants. After us, it will be the home of future generations. What we do now will decide whether it ends up a messy, overheated planet, or one that's healthy and safe to live on.

Index

Entries in **bold** refer to main subject entries. Entries in *italics* refer to illustrations

Acknowledgments

The publishers would like to thank the following sources for the use of their photographs:
Key: t = top, b = bottom, l = left, r = right, c = center, bg = background

Alamy 18 Craig Tuttle/Design Pics Inc; 21(bg) Lumoworks; 41 Paulo Oliveira; 64 imagebroker; 78–79 age footstock; 84–85 Jack Goldfarb/Design Pics Inc; 108–109 A & J Visage; 112–113(bg) Jim Reed; 117 blickwinkel; 122(b) Tom Uhlman; 126(t) Nature Picture Library/Alamy; 130(b) Arctic Images/Alamy Stock Photo; 133(b) AJSenviron/Alamy Stock Photo; 134–135(b) MARKA/Alamy; 140(t) Design Pics Inc/Alamy Stock Photo; 142(tl) Kpzfoto/Alamy Stock Photo; 148–149(t) Jeremy Sutton-Hibbert/Alamy Stock Photo; 153(c) David Wall/Alamy Stock Photo; 155(tr) Imagegallery2/Alamy Stock Photo

Dreamstime 23(tr) Mirkamoksha; 60(bl) Biolifepics; 68(cr) Bluesunphoto; 97(tr) Wickedgood; 101(bl) Astrofireball, (cr) Dreamstime; 115(cl) Naluphoto

EcoZone 141(tr) www.ecozone.co.uk

FLPA 36(bg) Phil McLean/FLPA; 37(tr) Michael & Patricia Fogden/Minden Pictures/FLPA; 62(bg) Tui De Roy/Minden Pictures; 64(c) Norbert Wu/Minden Pictures; 85(br) Yva Momatiuk & John Eastcott/Minden Pictures; 141(bl) ImageBroker; 148–149(bg) Katherine Feng

Fotolia.com 22(c) Konstantin Sutyagin; 29(t) Alexey Khromushin; 31(tl) Sharpshot, (cl) Anette Linnea Rasmus; 40(c) U.P.images; 74–75 (used throughout) Alexey Khromushin; 76(br) Sharpshot; 121(bl) schaltwerk; 138(bg) David Kesti; 144(t) steve estvanik; 146(bl) Lana; 152(bl) MiklG; 154(bg) Igor Bekirov

Getty 15(cr) Douglas Peebles/Corbis NX; 28(bg) Julie Deransky/Corbis Historical; 32(tr) Michael S. Yamashita/Corbis; 83(bg) Robert Holmes/Corbis Documentary; 110(cl) Michele Eve Sandberg; 121(cl) Bettmann; 123(cl) Getty Images AsiaPac/China Photos/Getty; 127(tr) Dean Conger/Corbis Historical, (br) Getty Images AsiaPac/Ryan Pierse/Getty; 131(br) Gideon Mendel/Corbis Documentary/Getty; 133(tr) Phil Schermeister/Corbis Historical/Getty; 134(b) Viviane Moos/Corbis Historical/Getty; 136(bg) David McNew, Getty Images North America/Getty; 137(br) John Dickson/Moment Open/Getty; 142(b) Christophe Simon/AFP/Getty; 143(tl) Martin Harvey/Corbis Documentary/Getty; 144(b) Per-Anders Pettersson/Getty Images News; 147(tl) Brian S. Turner/Corbis Documentary/Getty; 151(tl) Dimas Ardian/Stringer/Getty Images AsiaPac/Getty; 153(tr) Jeffrey L. Rotman/Corbis Documentary/Getty; 155(br) Bloomberg/Getty

Glow Images 81(cr) Heritage Images/Historica Graphica Collection

iStock 16 Lukáš Hejtman; 23(bg) IMPALASTOCK; 26(bg) weareadventurers; 46(br) Joshua Haviv; 64(bg) Miguel Angelo Silva; 72(b) brytta; 74(bl) David Mathies; 77(t) alohaspirit; 101(t) Scene_It; 102(b) Sean Randall; 115(tr) luoman; 119(br) micheldenijs; 122(tr) mateo69; 124(b) ra-photos; 125(br) AlbyDeTweede; 126(cr) joxxxjo; 131(tr) majorosl/iStock; 134–135(t) egdigital; 135(br) Sportstock; 137(tr) clintspencer, (cl) iStock; 145(b) dejan750/iStock; 147(br) iStock.com

Mint Images 156(bg) Mint Images/Frans Lanting/Getty

NASA 82(bl) NASA/JPL/UCSD/JSC; 112(t) Lori Losey; 113(cl) Jesse Allen, Earth Observatory, Image interpretation provided by Dave Santek and Jeff Key, University of Wisconsin-Madison; 116–117(bg) Provided by the SeaWiFS Project, NASA/Goddard Space Flight Center and ORBIMAGE

Nature Picture Library 62(br) bJurgen Freund; 64(tr) David Shale; 66(bg) Doug Perrine

Rex Features 89(l) KeystoneUSA-ZUMA

ShutterstockPremier back cover: (tc) Luna Vandoorne, (tr) EpicStockMedia, (bc) Oliver Klimek, (br) Dimitry Pichugin; 2–3 Dmitry Kulagin; 4–5 Dmitry Pichugin; 10(cr) Alexey Repka; 11(bl) Wild Arctic Pictures; 13(b) Sam Dcruz; 18(b) Jose Gil; 19(bg) Jarno Gonzalez Zarraonandia; 20(bg) Becky Stares; 24(br) yvon52; 25(cr) urosr, (bc) Crepesoles; 29(cl) Menna, (c) spirit of america, (cr) yankane; 31(tr) MarcelClemens, (br) douglas knight; 32(cl) Denis Selivanov; 35(tl) Oliver Klimek; 37(cl) Steve Bower; 38(bl) Vadim Petrakov; 39(bl) Willem Tims; 41(tl) Rich Carey; 42(tl) Krzysztof Odziomek, (bl) Cathy Keifer; 44(bg) Aubrey Laughlin, (c) ktsdesign; 48(tl) fashcool, (bl) Regien Paassen; 52(tr) agrosse; 54(bc) cynoclub, (c) Boris Pamikov, (bl) Lynsey Allan; 56(br) Ian Scott; 58(bl) Eric Isselee, (tr) Luna Vandoorne, (bg) Powell's Point; 60(bl) worldswildlifewonders, (tr) Vladimir Melnik, (bg) Mariusz Potocki; 62(bl) David Evison; 66(bg) foryouinf, (tl) AridOcean, (bl) Arto Hakola; 68(bl) Andrea Ricordi, (tr) Gail Johnson, (bl) Jenny Leonard, (br) Mariko Yuki; 70(cr) Steve Estvanik, (br) BMJ, (bg) Rich Lindie; 72(tr) DJTaylor, (tr) Mark Hall, (bl) ANCH; 74(cl) Seriousjoy, (b) Kevin Eaves, (br) Asaf Eliason; 75(trl) haveseen, (tr) Wild ArctiPictures, (c) Pichugin Dmitry, (cr) Oleg Znamenskiy, (bc) Tatiana Popova; 76(tr) Redsapphire; 78(bg) 1000 Words, (br) Mark Sayer, (tr) Morozova Oxana; 79(bl) Dmitriy Bryndin; 80–81(bg) Roberto Caucino; 81(tl) loskutnikov; 84(bl) Alexandr Zyryanov; 87(bl) Christy Nicholas; 88(t) Olivier Le Queinec, (br) Mike Buchheit; 90(t) Bull's-Eye Arts; 91(tr) Mikhail Pogosov, (b) Armin Rose, (tr) Brandelet; 92(tr) @cam; 93(bl) Stephen Meese; (br) Melissa Brandes, (br) Dustie, (br) Ortodox, (br) Slobodan Djajic, (cr) Robert Hoetink, (cr) photobank.kiev.ua, (cr) behindlens; (tr) Martin Preston, (tr) Vlue, (tr) Sinelyov, (tr) Tudor Spinu, (tr) Jennifer Griner; 94–95(bg) kornilov007; 95(tl) Jack Dagley Photography, (bc) Sam Dcruz, (cr) Gunnar Pippel; 99(br) javarman, (bl) DarkOne; 100(bg) PhotoHouse, (bl) pzAxe; 102(tr) EcoPrint; 103(t) outdoorsman, (bl) Jean-Edouard Rozey; 105(bl) Patryk Kosmider, (br) riekephotos; 106(bg) AdamEdwards; 107(b) Squarciomomo, (t) photomaster; 108(tr) Khirman Vladimir; 108–109(bc) Steve Mann; 109(ct) AISPIX by Image Source; 111(b) Map Resources; 113(cr) George Burba; 114(bg) Lee Prince; 125(tr) anweber

Science Photo Library 84–85(bg) Gary Hincks; 132(bg) Victor Habbick Visions

Wikimedia Commons 109(br) Olof Arenius

All other photographs are from: DigitalSTOCK, digitalvision, John Foxx, PhotoAlto, PhotoDisc, PhotoEssentials, PhotoPro, Stockbyte

Front cover artwork Stuart Jackson-Carter

All other artworks are from the Miles Kelly Artwork Bank

Every effort has been made to acknowledge the source and copyright holder of each picture. Miles Kelly Publishing apologizes for any unintentional errors or omissions.